Abundance

CITY FOOD FROM THE CAPE

Abundance

MARLENE VAN DER WESTHUIZEN

photography by Johan Wilke

BOOK**STORM**   MACMILLAN

Contents

CHAPTER 6

CHAPTER 7

CHAPTER 8

CHAPTER 9

CHAPTER 10

Coffee & thyme

Fork on Long

Street of gold

Market day

Sailor in my kitchen

Preface

*T*his exquisite city, with its abundance of colours and flavours, has always called with a slightly hoarse voice to those adventurous enough to hear her.

Early in our married lives we heard that call and so have spent most of our adult years in the shadow of Signal Hill, in Green Point village. I would love to show you these narrow streets and half-forgotten alleys that I so fiercely love.

I want you to look at the dominant sandstone mass that is Table Mountain, the rich indigenous fynbos, the sometimes-stormy lead-grey seas breaking onto powder-like beaches ringed with massive boulders. The blistering South-Easter that pushes a thick white cloud over the mountain and then leaves in its wake champagne-clear skies and calm aquamarine seas.

Cape Town is not about half-measures.

It is in this magnificent city – that sits down to a meal whenever it wants to – that we chose to make a life and raise a child. It is here, within walking distance from the Atlantic, that the first reluctant haircut was done by Theo the barber, the first hot chocolate was drunk at Giovanni's … and the first of numerous beers were quaffed at Pizzeria Napoletana.

In this book I want to share with you the part of Cape Town that we call home: from Sea Point to De Waterkant and the Bo Kaap, with a small swing through Bree, Loop and Long streets in town, followed by a peek at the goings-on in Woodstock and a bowl of spaghetti in Observatory. Perhaps a quick trot through the Neighbourhood Goods Market in Albert Road on a Saturday morning, accompanied by a glass of champagne and a plateful of freshly shucked West Coast oysters. A glimpse into a friend's home. A moody walk through thick mist on the Sea Point promenade.

And I want you to sit down at our table and share in the meals that we love to prepare. Rich duck soup, Pam's fish pie, lamb and date tagine, duck breast with blueberries, beef tongue with white wine and port sauce, St George's chicken and serranitos. All shared with loved ones and friends. A lifetime of wine and friendship.

I hope you love passing through as much as we do.

Our precious city.

Marlene

October 2012

chapter 1

Whisper horses

There is an urban myth – more of an instruction, really – that you should not fly out of Cape Town if you don't have the lingering taste of one of Aris Souvlaki's kebabs in your mouth. And that you should indulge in this spicy, meaty Greek deliciousness while walking through the salt-spray air down the Sea Point promenade, towards Kevin Brand's *White Horses*, my whisper horses.

Sea Point is where we took little boys for haircuts at Theo's, forced them through Sunday School, and taught them to swim in the iconic swimming pool. After that, of course, we needed to warm their freezing limbs with small glasses of creamy hot chocolate.

For years we have been sitting down for light lunches on the veranda at La Perla on Beach Road, and lately also at La Boheme on Main.

And on a night, roughly once a fortnight, when you need an excellent plate of nourishing food cooked by someone else, we find ourselves pushing aside the beaded curtain that is the portal to Piero Tarantello's Italian table at Pizzeria Napoletana, Main Road.

This wondrous family trattoria, more than 50 years later, still belongs to Gino and Maria Barletta. It is an institution … though many pillars of society are still slightly wary of the huge plastic crayfish of their childhood nightmares standing guard above the bar counter.

MUSIC FOR THIS CHAPTER: *Wild is the Wind* by Kellylee Evans
LEFT: *Original interior of the oldest family restaurant in Cape Town with Piero Tarantello, the host.*

- Hot drinking chocolate

- Cauliflower soup with walnut & Stilton toast

- Lentil salad with walnut oil

- Tomato & tapenade tartlets

- Calf's liver with lemon

- Pam's fish pie

- Veal limone

- Pork belly with lemon

- Garlic mash

- Mariaan's glorious pecan & coconut cake

Hot drinking chocolate

This is what I make on a wet, winter's day after a walk on the misty Sea Point promenade while ducking the spray of the massive waves. Then I cuddle in front of the fire, warming my icy hands around the cup.

Serves 6

- 800 ml full cream milk
- 250 g dark, creamy chocolate
- 2 cinnamon sticks
- ½ t ground cloves
- ½ t ground nutmeg
- wide strip of orange peel to taste
- 120 ml thick cream

Put the milk, chocolate, cinnamon, cloves, nutmeg and orange peel in a saucepan. Heat the mixture over a low heat, stirring all the time with a small whisk until the chocolate has melted and the chocolate cream is completely smooth and really hot.

Remove the cinnamon sticks and the orange peel, and pour the chocolate into small cups.

Spoon a dollop of the thick cream on top and sip some immediately!

Desserts are like mistresses. They are bad for you. So if you have one, you might as well have two.

CHEF ALAIN DUCASSE

Cooking is like love,
it should be entered into with
abandon or not at all.

HARRIET VON HORNE

Cauliflower soup WITH WALNUT & STILTON TOAST

Since regularly spending time in the little French village of Charroux I can never ignore any recipe that sports walnuts or walnut oil. The idea for this one popped out of an international food magazine in the form of a cutting a couple of years ago … and it is just lovely! And it translates very well to Cape Town shores!

Serves 6

- 1.25 kg cauliflower, broken into florets
- 50 ml extra virgin olive oil
- 1 T butter
- 3 leeks, chopped and rinsed well
- 3 cloves garlic, peeled and chopped
- 1.5 L chicken stock*
- 1 bouquet garni, made with sage, thyme and 2 bay leaves
- salt and white pepper to taste
- 60 ml walnut oil
- 2 shallots, peeled and chopped
- 2 T fresh sage leaves
- 6 slices rustic walnut bread
- 150 g Stilton cheese, at room temperature

Preheat the oven's grill. Heat the olive oil and butter in a heavy-based saucepan and add 1 kg of the cauliflower florets to the pan (save some for later). Gently toss with the olive oil and butter. Add the leeks, garlic, chicken stock and bouquet garni and cook over medium heat until the vegetables are tender. Remove the bouquet garni and discard.

Using a handheld liquidiser, process the soup until it has a gloriously creamy consistency. Season to taste and keep warm.

Meanwhile, heat 40 ml of the walnut oil in a small frying pan over medium heat. Add the shallots and the sage to the pan. Cut the rest of the cauliflower into thin slices and add to the pan. Cook until crisp and season.

Place the slices of walnut bread on a roasting pan and slip under the heated grill. Toast on both sides, remove and drizzle with the rest of the walnut oil. Spread the Stilton cheese on the hot toast.

Ladle the hot soup into warmed soup bowls, spoon some of the crisp cauliflower and sage mixture into each plate and serve with a slice of the Stilton toast.

*See recipe on page 71.

TOP: *Early morning at Sea Point swimming pool.*

Lentil salad WITH WALNUT OIL

Living very close to Le Puy in the Auvergne, I love cooking with the lovely green lentils that we find here.
This is a delicious salad that we often serve with lamb.

Serves 6

- 350 g lentils
- 1 bouquet garni made with leek, parsley, rosemary, thyme, sage and 2 bay leaves
- 2 cloves garlic, peeled
- salt to taste
- 1 T olive oil
- 3 shallots, peeled and chopped
- 2 T walnut oil
- 1 T smooth, creamy mustard
- 2 T flat-leaf parsley, chopped
- 125 g walnuts, roasted and chopped
- 6 slices Parma ham, grilled to a crisp
- 6 eggs, poached until soft

Wash the lentils in a colander, drain and place in a saucepan with the bouquet garni and garlic. Cover the lentils with cold water, add a little salt, bring to a gentle simmer and cook until soft. Drain, discard the bouquet garni, and keep the lentils warm.

In the meantime, heat the olive oil in a small pan and fry the shallots until translucent and lightly cooked. Fold the shallots into the lentils.

Whisk the walnut oil and mustard together, add the parsley and fold, with the walnuts, into the lentils.

To serve, spoon the lentils onto serving plates and garnish with the crisp Parma ham. Drop a warm poached egg on top and season to taste.

Serve immediately.

ABOVE: *Morning on the Sea Point promenade.*

Tomato & tapenade tartlets

This is an old favourite. Terribly easy with serious clout! To be served al fresco … in our case it will be under the pomegranate tree in the courtyard.

Serves 6

- 1 roll of puff pastry, defrosted
- 1 t butter
- 1 egg white
- 250 g tapenade, made of black olives
- 30 baby tomatoes, halved lengthwise
- 250 g feta cheese, crumbled
- 6 anchovies
- sprig fresh thyme

Preheat the oven to 200 deg C/Gas 6.

Roll out the pastry and cut into rounds with a pastry cutter. Line six individually buttered ramekins. Prick tiny holes with a fork in the pastry and brush the pastry with a little egg white. This will ensure that the pastry will be fabulously crisp.

Spoon a dollop of the tapenade into the pastry case, spread slightly with a fork, crumble the feta over the tapenade and spoon an anchovy onto each little tart. Pack the tomatoes in tight formation onto the tapenade-and-feta mix and bake immediately for about 25 minutes or until the pastry has turned a lovely caramel colour.

Garnish with a sprig of fresh thyme and serve with a fresh rocket salad.

ABOVE LEFT: Dragonfly Girl *by Marieke Prinsloo-Rowe on Sea Point promenade.*
ABOVE RIGHT: *The first haircut.*

ABOVE: *Souvlaki to go?*

Calf's liver WITH LEMON

I am having a very serious thought that calf's liver cooked in this way may be even better than foie gras. Try it!

Serves 6

- 2 cloves garlic, peeled and sliced
- handful fresh parsley, chopped
- 60 g butter
- 3 slices calf's liver
- juice of 1 lemon

Chop the garlic and the parsley together and sauté gently in the butter over a very low heat. Take care not to burn the garlic. Remove the mixture from the pan with a slotted spoon.

Reheat the pan juices and quickly fry the slices of liver in the same butter.

Do not overcook the liver.

It is at its best when it is slightly pink when you cut it. Remove the liver from the pan and slice into thin slivers. Deglaze the juices with the lemon juice and spoon the sauce over the liver slivers.

Serve immediately as a snack.

Salt is born from the purest of parents: the sun and the sea.

PYTHAGORAS

TOP: *Open air gym in Sea Point.*
BELOW: White Horses *by Kevin Brand.*

Pam's fish pie

A couple of years ago at a friend's birthday party in the UK, the most delicious fish pie I have ever tasted was served for breakfast the morning after. This might quite possibly be the closest I'll ever get to recreating that fabulous creamy dish. With the help of Pam … again! This is such a good homecoming dish on those grey winter Cape days when the rain is sweeping across Table Bay.

Serves 8

- 1.5 kg floury potatoes, peeled
- salt
- 200 g butter
- ½ t freshly grated nutmeg
- 125 ml full cream
- 50 g flour
- 350 ml milk
- handful parsley, chopped
- handful dill, chopped
- 2 cloves garlic, peeled and chopped
- 1 t white pepper*
- 350 g smoked haddock, boneless and cubed
- 250 g fresh salmon, boneless and cubed
- 250 g hake, boneless and cubed
- 8 eggs, medium boiled, peeled and gently quartered

Preheat the oven to 200 deg C/Gas 6.

Cook the potatoes in salted water until soft, then drain. Mash the potatoes together with 100 g butter until it has a creamy consistency. Add the nutmeg and fold in the cream. Taste and season. Keep the creamy mash in the warm pot until you need it.

In the meantime, melt 75 g of the butter in a small saucepan, add the flour and stir vigorously until it forms a thick paste. Add the milk gradually to the roux while you keep on stirring until you have a fabulously creamy béchamel.

Fold the parsley, dill and garlic into the sauce and season with some white pepper only.

Butter a deep ovenproof dish with the remaining butter.

Arrange the cubed fish and the quartered eggs in the dish and spoon the lovely hot sauce over the mixture.

Top with the creamy mash and bake for 35 – 40 minutes or until the potato is nicely browned.

Serve as soon as possible!

* The smoked haddock will quite possibly be salty enough to season the pie.

ABOVE: *Gatepost to the Three Anchor Bay rectory.*

Veal limone

Without doubt one of my absolutely favourite dishes. And the only thing I always order when my husband and I go to our 'local' in Sea Point … this best kept secret in town is also one of the oldest Italian restaurants in Main Road. Once you have been allowed entry through the beaded curtain at the front door into the packed little trattoria, you will enjoy a plateful of some of the best food I have ever eaten.
Serves 4

- 12 veal scaloppine, thinly pounded
- 1 T flour
- 2 T extra virgin olive oil
- 1 T butter
- 200 ml dry white wine
- 100 ml lemon juice
- 300 ml chicken stock*
- 3 T flat-leaf parsley, chopped
- salt and freshly ground black pepper

Toss the slices of veal lightly in the flour, shaking off the excess.

Heat the olive oil in a saucepan, add 1 teaspoon of the butter and melt over a high heat. Fry the veal scaloppine very quickly in the hot pan. Place the meat on a lovely serving dish and keep warm.

Deglaze the pan with the white wine, making sure that you scrape up all the tasty brown bits. Add the lemon juice and the chicken stock, and reduce the liquid until it has a fabulously creamy consistency. Add the rest of the cold butter and stir it quickly through the sauce. Taste and season with salt and a generous turn of the pepper grinder.

Spoon the sauce over the meat and garnish with the parsley. Serve with a platter full of freshly boiled tagliolini** that you have tossed with lashings of olive oil.

This is so good!

* See recipe on page 71.
** Or serve with a pasta of your choice.

LEFT TOP: *La Perla opposite the Sea Point Pavilion.*
LEFT MIDDLE: *Piero behind the bar.*
LEFT BOTTOM: *Pizzeria Napoletana.*

Pork belly WITH LEMON

There is just nothing like the combination of this fabulously crispy pork belly and the creamy garlic mash. It is a very good idea to make enough for all the neighbours … and to make sure that everyone you were planning to see the next day has been invited to the feast! A brisk walk on the Sea Point promenade after the meal might also be a good idea …
Serves 8

- 2 kg pork belly, scored
- 2 T extra virgin olive oil
- juice of 1 lemon
- 1 T sage, finely chopped
- 6 garlic cloves, finely chopped
- 1 T salt
- 1 T freshly ground black pepper

Preheat the oven to 200 deg C/Gas 6.

Combine the olive oil, lemon juice, sage, garlic, salt and pepper in a small bowl. Rub the mixture all over the pork skin and into the slits in the skin.

Place the pork on a wire rack on a tray and slide into the middle of the hot oven. Roast the meat for about 30 minutes or until the skin begins to form into a lovely caramelised crackle.

Reduce the oven temperature to about 180 deg C/Gas 4 and allow the meat to cook for another hour or until it is deliciously tender.

Slice the pork into thin slices and serve with the fragrant garlic mash.

Garlic mash

- 2 whole heads of garlic
- 1.5 kg mashing potatoes, peeled and cubed
- 150 g butter (or more!)
- 50 ml extra virgin olive oil
- salt to taste

Preheat the oven to 180 deg C/Gas 4.

Lop the top off each garlic head, drizzle with a little of the olive oil and wrap them in foil. Place the garlic heads in a small ovenproof dish and pop them into the oven for about 40 minutes. (Sometimes I just put the garlic in the oven with the pork.)

Boil the potatoes in a saucepan of water for about 15 minutes until tender.

Drain the potatoes and mash them until utterly creamy.

Remove the absolutely tender garlic from the oven and squeeze the pulp into the mash. Add the butter and the rest of the olive oil, and cream together with a large spoon. Taste the mash and season lightly.

Serve with the pork belly.

ABOVE: *Beautiful architectural lines in Sea Point.*

ABOVE: *Three Anchor Bay Dutch Reformed Church and bell.*

Mariaan's glorious pecan & coconut cake

As a child growing up in Sasolburg and later as a student in Pretoria, this was possibly the one cake that was not left standing. And if no one was watching, some sneaking off of the fabulous coconut cream was always done!

Serves 10

- 500 g cake flour
- 250 g castor sugar
- 4 t baking powder
- 1 t salt
- 125 g soft butter
- 1 t almond extract
- 250 ml milk
- 3 egg whites, whipped until stiff peaks form

CREAMY COCONUT FILLING

- 250 g castor sugar
- 250 ml evaporated milk
- 3 egg yolks, slightly beaten
- 125 g butter, soft
- 1 t vanilla paste
- 250 g desiccated coconut
- 125 g pecan nuts, gently roasted and chopped

Heat the oven to 180 deg/Gas 4.

In a large mixing bowl, sift together the flour, sugar, baking powder and salt. Add the butter and mix very well for at least 4 minutes. Slowly add the almond extract and the milk while mixing.

Gently fold in the egg whites and spoon the mixture into two well-buttered, loose-bottomed (why do I so love this description?) cake pans.

Bake the cakes for about 30 minutes or until a skewer comes out clean. Once they are done, remove the cakes from the oven and allow them to cool down in the cake pans before up-ending them onto a wire rack.

To make the fabulous filling, place the sugar, evaporated milk, egg yolks and butter into a medium-sized pan and bring to a gentle simmer. Keep stirring the mixture until it thickens to a lovely creamy consistency. Remove the pan from the heat and add the vanilla. Spoon the coconut and the pecan nuts into the mixture and fold through thoroughly.

Allow the mixture to cool down completely before spreading half the filling onto the first cake. Place the second cake on top and spoon the rest of the filling over the cake.

Eat as quickly as possible!

chapter 2

A grain of salt

A nd this is where we live. In a jewellery box of a little home, among tassels, polished brass, velvet curtains tied back with thick cords, towers of slightly dusty books and handed-down kitchenware.

This is the quiet-eye-of-the-storm that we all need. That comforting armchair that has, over many years, moulded itself to the shape of your limbs. Where you can rest your travel-weary bones.

Here we gather on Sunday afternoons around the bleached wooden table next to the fountain under the pomegranate tree, telling the tales that make up the fabric of lives shared.

There is something compelling about rich pea soup ladled into a hand-painted Suzy Cooper bowl, or the ritual of carrying a large pewter platter of steaming, creamy polenta and a stew of garlicky chicken towards the massive yellowwood dining table. This will always be a small spiritual homecoming: the pop of a cork, the sound of wine being poured, while from the depths of the old house sounds the familiar laughter of a dear friend.

Small pleasures. Life.

MUSIC FOR THIS CHAPTER: *Our Love is Easy* by Melody Gardot
OPPOSITE: *The fountain in our garden.*

- Pea soup

- Serranitos

- Fresh fig & blue cheese salad

- Tomato salad with walnuts, walnut oil & thyme

- St George's chicken with pancetta & capers

- Tuna & rice

- Braised lamb shanks with roasted shallots

- Clyde apple pie

- Coffee & chocolate pots

Pea soup

During the wonderfully, misty and wet winter months in Cape Town, you always need a warm bowl of soup.
And a well-made pea soup is just so good!

Serves 6

- 500 g green split peas, soaked overnight
- 75 ml extra virgin olive oil
- 1 T duck fat
- 1 T butter
- 1 ham hock
- 2 pork trotters
- 250 g bacon, cut into small bits
- 4 leeks, washed and chopped finely
- 4 garlic cloves, chopped
- 1 stick celery with leaves, chopped finely
- 2 large potatoes, peeled and cubed
- 1 bouquet garni, made with sage, thyme, parsley and a bay leaf
- 2 L chicken stock*
- salt and white pepper to taste

Heat the olive oil, duck fat and butter in a large soup pot. Brown the ham hock, trotters and bacon before adding the drained split peas, leeks, garlic, celery, potatoes, bouquet garni and chicken stock to the pot.

Simmer over a medium heat for about 2 hours, regularly removing the foam that forms on the broth with a slotted spoon. You may add water to the broth if necessary.

Once the meat is so tender that it falls from the bones, scoop it out of the soup, allow it to cool a little and debone it carefully. Use your fingers and shred the meat into small bite-sized pieces.

Spoon half of the broth into a food processor and liquidise. Return the thick purée to the soup pot and stir it into the broth. Add the shredded meat, taste and season with quite a heavy hand on the pepper pot!

Spoon the soup into a warmed soup tureen and serve with fresh crusty bread.

* See recipe on page 71.

OPPOSITE BOTTOM: *Ex-Trovato House reading chair.*
RIGHT TOP: *Dining room chair detail.*
RIGHT: *A glimpse into the snug.*

Have nothing in your house
that you do not know to
be useful, or believe to be
beautiful.

WILLIAM MORRIS

Serranitos

A meal best served often … and specifically to boys!
We love it.

Serves 6

- 3 pork fillets, cut into 8 slices each and flattened with the flat side of a chef's knife
- 6 garlic cloves, crushed to a paste
- 1 T paprika
- 1 t white pepper
- 150 ml olive oil
- 4 green peppers, grilled, seeded and peeled
- 6 T creamy mayonnaise
- 12 slices of ciabatta, toasted
- 12 thinly sliced Parma ham*
- salt and freshly ground black pepper to taste

In a small bowl, mix the garlic, paprika and white pepper together. Roll the slices of meat in the mixture and allow to marinate for about 30 minutes.

In the meantime, heat some of the olive oil in a saucepan. Slice the peeled green peppers into thin strips and quickly fry them in the hot oil. Season and set aside.

Spread a dollop of mayonnaise on 6 of the toasted ciabatta slices. Place 2 slices of Parma ham on each of these toasts.

Add the remaining olive oil to the saucepan and when it begins to smoke, add the pork slices and quickly fry for 1 minute before turning over and frying the other side. Transfer the pork slices onto the ciabatta slices, followed by a slice of green pepper. Pour a little of the warm olive oil on top and season to taste.

Cover with the second slice of ciabatta and enjoy!

This is absolutely best eaten with your hands … keep a huge napkin ready. And please have this with an ice-cold beer.

* Traditionally, Serranitos are made with Spanish Serrano ham.

TOP: *Water bottles bought at the Victoria Falls Hotel.*

Fresh fig & blue cheese salad

The first sign of imminent autumn must be the honey-sweet sun-ripened figs of the Cape. How we do love them!

Serves 6

- 300 g blue cheese*
- 12 large ripe figs, sun-warmed
- a large handful watercress, stemmed

DRESSING
- 2 T extra virgin olive oil
- 2 T dry sherry
- 2 t chives, chopped finely
- 2 t parsley, chopped finely
- 2 t chervil, chopped finely
- 1 clove garlic, chopped finely
- salt and freshly ground black pepper

Preheat the oven to 180 deg C/Gas 4.

Cut the cheese into slices and place them on an oven tray. Slip the tray into the oven for about 4 minutes. The cheese must be just slightly warmed.

Arrange the watercress on a salad platter. Gently tear the figs apart with your fingers and scatter the pieces over and into the watercress. Using a spatula, slide the warm cheese slices onto the salad. Spoon lashings of the lovely French dressing over everything and serve immediately.

DRESSING
Whisk all the ingredients together in a small bowl.

Season to taste.

* I love the bite of a ripe Roquefort but any blue cheese of your choice will do.

LEFT: *A glimpse through the window into my pantry.*
RIGHT: *Our casserole dish from Kopenhagen, the Smithfield family farm.*

Tomato salad WITH WALNUTS, WALNUT OIL & THYME

I absolutely adore sun-ripened tomatoes and my son has started to serve them with those divine soft sprigs of young thyme that you pick in late spring. We are all hooked on this salad!

Serves 6

- 8 ripe tomatoes, cut into wedges
- handful fresh thyme, chopped
- 3 T walnuts, toasted
- 2 T walnut oil
- 2 T extra virgin olive oil
- juice of I lime
- I t honey
- salt and freshly ground black pepper

Place the tomatoes in a serving dish. Toss the tomatoes with the thyme and walnuts.

Whisk the walnut oil, olive oil, lime and honey together and season the mixture lightly.

Sprinkle the dressing over the salad and serve.

RIGHT: *The fountain in our garden.*

I can't stand people who don't take their food seriously.

OSCAR WILDE

St George's chicken WITH PANCETTA & CAPERS

A very easy and utterly sumptuous chicken dish. I always serve this with creamy polenta … in large soup plates!

Serves 6

- 6 chicken drumsticks
- 6 chicken thighs
- 3 T extra virgin olive oil
- 1 T butter
- 150 g pancetta, diced
- 75 g small capers
- 4 cloves garlic, peeled and chopped
- 1 bouquet garni, made with rosemary, parsley, thyme and 2 bay leaves
- 500 ml dry white wine
- 500 ml chicken stock*
- salt and freshly ground black pepper
- handful fresh sage leaves

* See recipe on page 71.

Melt the butter in 2 T of the olive oil, using a large, heavy-based saucepan.

Toss the pancetta in the oil mixture over medium heat until the fat begins to render. Add the chicken pieces to the pan and brown. Add the capers, garlic, bouquet garni and the wine, and bring to a gentle simmer for about 15 minutes before adding the stock.

Cook the chicken for another 40 minutes or until it is completely tender and the liquid has reduced to a creamy consistency. Season to taste.

In the meantime, heat the rest of the olive oil in a warm pan and toss the sage leaves very quickly in the hot oil. Remove the crisp leaves with a fork and drain on a piece of kitchen paper.

Remove the chicken from the saucepan and place in a lovely serving dish. Remove the bouquet garni. Spoon the pancetta and the capers, as well as the sauce, over the chicken.

Garnish with the crisp sage leaves and serve with a steaming platter of creamy polenta.

RIGHT: *Garden table underneath the pomegranate tree.*

Tuna & rice

This is a real old family standby. Ideal for those quick Friday night dinners before the kids head out to Long Street!

Serves 6

- 500 g tinned tuna, drained*
- 1 T extra virgin olive oil
- 2 brown onions, peeled and chopped finely
- 1 red pepper, seeded and chopped finely
- 2 T butter
- 2 T flour
- 350 ml milk
- 1 T fresh thyme, chopped
- 2 t paprika
- salt and freshly ground black pepper
- 500 g cooked white rice

Heat the olive oil in a small saucepan and braise the onion and red pepper in the oil until translucent but not browned.

Melt the butter in a medium saucepan and add the flour. Stir vigorously while adding the milk. Keep stirring until you have a lovely creamy, thick white sauce. Add the drained tuna bits as well as the onion, red pepper, thyme and paprika.

Fold the ingredients together, taste and season before serving immediately with some steaming white rice. A glass of white wine will also not go to waste!

* I prefer using tuna that has been preserved in oil.

ABOVE: *Home cellar.*

One cannot think well, love well, sleep well, if one has not dined well.

VIRGINIA WOOLF

Braised lamb shanks WITH ROASTED SHALLOTS

This is the perfect winter's dish. And I adore serving this with a really creamy garlicky mash.

Serves 6

- 6 lamb shanks, French-trimmed
- 1 T duck fat
- 3 carrots, peeled and julienned
- 4 leeks, sliced into pennies and rinsed
- 1 stick of celery, chopped
- 1 whole head of garlic, peeled
- salt and freshly ground pepper to taste
- 1 bottle of white wine
- 2 L chicken stock*
- 12 shallots, oven-roasted, to serve

Melt the duck fat in a flameproof casserole dish and braise the lamb shanks until nicely browned. Add the carrots, leeks, celery and garlic. Season lightly. Pour the white wine over all the ingredients and bring to a rapid boil. Allow all the alcohol to evaporate before adding the chicken stock. Gently simmer the shanks for about 2 hours or until the meat is almost falling from the bone.

Remove the shanks from the casserole dish and reduce the remaining stock until it has a sauce-like consistency.

Serve the lamb shanks on top of a scoop of buttery garlic mash with a roasted shallot or two. This is delicious!

* See recipe on page 71.

ABOVE: *Down at the garden gate.*

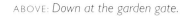

Clyde apple pie

A good apple pie is a thing of complete beauty. I love the tartness of the apples intermingling with the sweetness of the sultanas ... with a whiff of cinnamon hovering like a favourite granny's spirit.

Serves 8

PIE CRUMBLE

- 125 g butter
- 125 g castor sugar
- 1 egg
- 500 ml self-raising flour

FILLING

- 200 g sultanas
- 75 ml brandy
- 8 Granny Smith apples, peeled, cored and cut into thick slices
- 140 g castor sugar
- 2 T butter
- 250 ml water
- 1 t ground cinnamon
- ½ t grated nutmeg
- 100 g pecans, chopped

Knead all the pie crumble ingredients together into a soft ball. Wrap the dough in a piece of wax paper and keep it in the fridge until you need it.

FILLING

Soak the sultanas in the brandy overnight.

Heat the oven to 180 deg C/Gas 4.

Bring the apples, sugar, butter and water to a gentle simmer in a medium-sized pan. Add the sultanas and the brandy, as well as the cinnamon and nutmeg. Simmer the apples for about 10 minutes or until they are slightly cooked but still firm and the liquid has reduced to a syrup. Fold the pecans into the mixture.

Spoon the apple filling into a buttered pie dish.

Take the dough out of the fridge and grate it roughly and quite thickly over the apple pie filling.

Bake the pie in the hot oven until the crust is a fabulous caramel colour and quite crispy.

Serve warm with a dollop of thick cream or a scoop of the best vanilla ice-cream you can lay your hands on.

This is just so good!

TOP: *Kitchen art and fresh produce.*
MIDDLE: *Hunting trophies on the landing.*
BOTTOM: *Lizzies in Ouma Hester's retro vase.*

On the edge, over the edge, go over, find it, think it. Let it fill you and make you bleed with desire.

MARY RORICH

Coffee & chocolate pots

Something sweet and easy. I love serving these if we dine al fresco beneath the large pomegranate tree down in the garden. It is a no fuss dessert with maximum impact!

Serves 6

- 100 ml coffee, brewed really strong
- 3 T excellent Cognac or brandy
- 200 g dark chocolate*
- 250 ml thick cream
- 2 eggs

In a medium bowl mix the hot, just-made coffee and Cognac. Break the chocolate into bits and add to the coffee mixture. Whisk until smooth.

In a small saucepan, bring the cream to a slow simmer before pouring it into the chocolate mixture. Fold together gently and pour the mixture into six individual serving glasses. Allow to cool slightly before whisking in the eggs.

Leave the chocolate pots to set overnight in the fridge.

Serve with a dollop of thick cream and a sprinkling of cocoa powder.

* I prefer using the soft-centred slabs of chocolate.

OPPOSITE: *Moroccan peacock jewel box in front of a Zwelethu Mthethwa pastel.*
RIGHT: *Flowers with Walter Meyer's painting of Hylton Nel's garden in Bethulie as backdrop.*
ABOVE: *Original brass Victorian door knocker.*

chapter 3

The morning swim

There is a timelessness to life in Green Point village. There is the early call of the seagulls to hustle you out of bed. The energetic walk down to the untamed stretch of beach next to the promenade. And the breathless wade into the icy waves for a really bracing swim. The cup of creamy coffee at Gran's in Clyde Road. The gentle trundle up the hill with the morning paper under your arm. The hoarse call of ducks flying overhead.

In the early evening, locals gather on your stoep, a glass of chilled Semillon at each elbow, while you quickly throw together a platter of spaghetti and smoked oysters to share.

And hovering among us are the nimble spirits of the giants who have walked these narrow lanes. From Jan Rabie to Ingrid Jonker and – for too short a while – the wonderfully eccentric Scottish gentleman, Peter Shand Kydd, who left a cloud of cigar smoke in his wake.

In this village we live with our neighbours. We share in the first wobbly steps of our small children and in the gentle passing on of long-familiar faces.

This is home.

MUSIC FOR THIS CHAPTER: *Ta cigarette après l'amour* by Charles Dumont

- Marinated crottin

- Spaghetti with oysters

- Salmon rillette

- Green bean, pancetta & poached egg salad

- Hake with pesto, asparagus & tomato salad

- Chicken with ginger & chillies

- Fillet with tapenade

- Berry frangipane

- Honey & cheese cake

Marinated crottin

This is a lovely appetiser to serve with a glass of wine and a small slice of crusty bread.

Serves 6

- 6 slices Crottin* cheese, sliced in rounds
- 4 cloves
- 1 t coriander seeds
- 2 whole star anise
- 2 bay leaves
- 2 sprigs lemon thyme
- 1 sprig rosemary
- 8 juniper berries
- extra virgin olive oil

Place the slices of Crottin cheese in a small bowl with the herbs and spices. Fill the bowl with enough olive oil to cover the cheese and leave to marinate for 12 hours before serving with some fresh, crusty bread and a glass of ice-cold white wine.

* A strong-flavoured, small and hard goat's milk cheese from the Loire Valley, which is now also available in South Africa.

TOP: *Lion's Head at dawn.*
ABOVE: *Calm seas at high tide.*

Spaghetti with oysters

An Atlantic coast variation of a very easy pasta dish!
I love serving this on a large platter with a bottle or two of chilled rosé.

Serves 6

- 250 g smoked oysters
- 50 ml extra virgin olive oil
- 1 T chives, chopped finely
- 500 g spaghetti, dry
- 1 T salt
- salt and white pepper to taste
- handful wild rocket
- 100 g salmon caviar

In a small saucepan toss the smoked oysters quickly in the olive oil over a medium heat.

Add the chives.

Cook the pasta in boiling salted water, drain and toss quickly with the warm oysters.

Season to taste with the salt and white pepper.

Serve in warm pasta plates or bowls on top of a sprinkling of rocket. Garnish with a spoonful of salmon caviar.

Everything you see I owe to spaghetti.

SOPHIA LOREN

Food should be honest and humble,
reaching for greatness, not greedy with
pretension but pretending each time to be
like a lover's first kiss, a friend's comfort,
a loved one's reassurance, a tomorrow's
hope and a yesterday of no regrets.

JOHN JACKSON

Salmon rillette

A really tasty morsel — something you can whip together for a lovely sundowner on Clifton beach.

Serves 8

- 300 g salmon fillet, fresh
- juice of 1 lemon
- 150 g smoked salmon
- 1 T dill, chopped finely
- 250 g crème fraîche
- 100 g mayonnaise
- 1 t horseradish, creamed
- 4 spring onions, chopped finely
- salt and freshly ground black pepper to taste

ABOVE: *Living in Green Point.*

Preheat the oven to 180 deg C/Gas 4.

Pour half the lemon juice over the salmon fillet and season lightly. Cover the salmon and bake in the heated oven for about 15 minutes.

Remove from the oven and break the flesh into chunks, removing any bones that you may find.*

In the meantime, shred the smoked salmon and place it in a large mixing bowl, together with the dill, remaining lemon juice, crème fraîche, mayonnaise and horseradish. Using a fork, mix all the ingredients together quite vigorously until the mixture forms a lovely creamy paste.

Add the fresh salmon and repeat the process. (I enjoy the slight chunkiness!)

Spoon into a bowl, cover and keep in the fridge until you serve it. It is very good with some toast, garnished with the spring onions and a small gherkin on the side!

* I like using the skin as well but this is optional.

Green bean, pancetta & poached egg salad

Having the luxury of breaking the egg yolk and allowing it to drench this salad is just the ticket!

Serves 6

- 400 g young green beans, topped
- 300 g shelled peas
- 150 g macadamia nuts, roasted
- 150 ml extra virgin olive oil
- handful wild rocket
- 6 eggs, poached
- salt and freshly ground black pepper
- 12 slices pancetta, grilled until crisp

Place the beans and peas in a bowl, pour some boiling water over them and leave for about 8 minutes. Drain and then toss with the macadamia nuts and a little olive oil.

Arrange the rocket on 6 individual plates. Place an equal amount of green beans, peas and nuts on each of the plates.

To get the rustic 'paper package' look when doing a delicious version of a poached egg, simply drop each raw egg into a lightly olive-oiled square of plastic wrap that has been placed in a muffin pan. Tie each square with a piece of string and suspend from a wooden spoon into boiling water until cooked but still soft. Use a pair of scissors to slip the warm eggs onto the fresh salad. Season and garnish with shards of pancetta.

Enjoy immediately.

TOP RIGHT AND BELOW: *Gran's Coffee Shoppe in Clyde Road.*

Hake with pesto, asparagus & tomato salad

Living in such close proximity to the sea, we obviously enjoy a fair amount of fish. Hake is such an underestimated variety … I love the soft flakiness of the fish as well as the 'cleanness' of the dish.

Serves 6

- 6 hake fillets
- 150 ml extra virgin olive oil
- freshly made basil pesto*
- 500 g green asparagus, rinsed well
- 3 ripe tomatoes, sliced in wedges
- salt and freshly ground black pepper to taste
- handful rocket, washed

ABOVE: *Exhilarating morning swim in Green Point.*

Heat 50 ml of the olive oil in a saucepan over medium heat, and fry the fish gently and slowly on each side until it has been cooked to perfection. Remove from the pan, season and keep warm.

In the meantime, make the creamy basil pesto.* Spoon the pesto into a small bowl and keep aside.

Pour some boiling water over the asparagus and allow it to stand for about 3 minutes. Drain the asparagus and then toss gently with the tomatoes and the rest of the olive oil. Season to taste.

Arrange a little of the rocket on individual plates and top with the asparagus and tomatoes. Place a portion of hake next to the salad on each plate, with a dollop of basil pesto on the side.

Serve immediately.

* See pesto recipe on page 171.

Chicken with ginger & chillies

This is a seriously hot, hot chicken — enjoy with a glass or a bottle of cold Sauvignon Blanc.

Serves 6

- 1 large free-range chicken
- 50 g butter
- juice of 2 lemons
- 6 cm fresh ginger, peeled and chopped
- 4 cloves garlic, peeled and chopped
- 4 fresh, really hot green chillies, chopped
- 2 T extra virgin olive oil
- 1 t ground cumin
- 4 cardamom pods, peeled
- 1 t ground coriander
- salt and freshly ground black pepper

Using a sharp knife, make 2 deep diagonal slits in each chicken breast, going all the way to the bone. Do the same on the thighs and drumsticks. Place the chicken, breast up, in a roasting tin lined with a very large sheet of heavy foil that can eventually enclose the bird. Rub the butter into the slits.

Put the lemon juice, ginger, garlic, chillies, olive oil, cumin, cardamom and coriander in a blender and blend to a paste. Rub the mixture all over the chicken, inside and out. And please make sure that you avoid reacting to all urges to rub your eyes until after you have washed your hands really well!

Set aside for 30 minutes. Meanwhile, preheat the oven to 200 deg C/Gas 6. Dust the chicken with salt and black pepper. Fold the foil over the chicken so that the bird is completely enclosed. Place the roasting pan in the middle of the oven and roast the chicken for an hour. Open the foil regularly for the first 20 minutes and baste with the accumulated juices.

Once the chicken is roasted to perfection, remove it from the oven, carve into portions and serve on a large platter with basmati rice and baked sweet potatoes.

RIGHT: *Sumptuous city life.*

Fillet with tapenade

And then we have the fillet …

Serves 8

- 1.2 kg beef fillet, trimmed and cleaned
- 4 T extra virgin olive oil
- 2 T goose or duck fat
- 125 ml white wine
- salt and pepper
- 400 g tapenade, made from black olives
- 3 anchovies per person
- basil to garnish

Heat the olive oil and goose or duck fat in a pan and fry the fillet about 5 minutes on each side. Remove the fillet from the heat and allow to rest for about 20 minutes.

Deglaze the pan juices with the white wine. Reduce the pan juices to just cover the pan.

Slice the fillet into thick serving portions and reheat them quickly in the pan juices.

Remove the meat from the heat, season to taste and spoon a dollop of tapenade on top of each fillet.

Plate each serving individually, garnish with the anchovies and the basil and serve immediately with some greens.

TOP: *Quiet bedroom.*
LEFT: *Victorian paper weights.*
ABOVE: *Hats are made for walking.*

Berry frangipane

This dessert happened one evening when I suddenly had to rustle up something sweet. How fabulously simple!

Serves 6

- 1 roll puff pastry, defrosted
- 125 g almonds, ground
- 125 g castor sugar
- 75 ml cream
- 1 egg
- 250 g blueberries

Heat the oven to 200 deg C/Gas 6.

Smooth the pastry into 6 individual, buttered flan dishes. Prick the dough lightly with a fork.

Whisk the ground almonds, 75 g of the sugar, the cream and the egg together in a small mixing bowl. Spoon the mixture into the pastry cases. Divide about half of the berries between the individual desserts and put them into the hot oven. Bake for about 25 minutes or until the pastry has a lovely caramel colour.

Melt the rest of the sugar with 1 T water in a small pan. Reduce slightly until it has a syrupy consistency.

Remove the tarts from the oven, scoop them out of the moulds and place each on a small, pretty plate.

Drop the rest of the berries into the syrup, give them a quick turn and immediately spoon them onto the tarts.

Serve with some of the leftover syrup.

TOP: *A very popular mode of transport!*
LEFT: *Green Point street sign.*
MIDDLE: *Historic post box corner of Main and Clyde.*
ABOVE: *Retro car.*

Honey & cheese cake

This is a family recipe that has become one of my son's favourites. My mother had to bake this for his 21st birthday, to the huge pleasure of the crowd of guests!

Serves 8

- 75 g butter, room temperature
- 250 g castor sugar
- 3 eggs
- 350 g self-raising flour
- 1 t vanilla paste
- 175 ml full cream milk
- 250 g cheddar cheese, finely grated

SAUCE
- 150 ml honey
- 75 g butter

Preheat the oven to 180 deg C/Gas 4.

Butter a standard-sized ovenproof baking dish.

Whisk the butter and the sugar until it is light and foamy. Add the eggs and whisk well. Sift the flour into the mixture, add the vanilla and pour the milk into the batter while you are whisking it.

Bake the cake for about 25 minutes or until a skewer comes out clean.

TO MAKE THE SAUCE

Spoon the honey into the butter in a saucepan and heat together until they have melted and formed a lovely, glossy sauce. Remove from the heat.

Remove the cake from the oven, pour the piping hot sauce over it and cover with the grated cheese.

Eat immediately. This is utterly delicious!

ABOVE: *Copper pots carried personally from Dijon, France.*

chapter 4

True at first light

I'm not sure Hemingway had the soft morning Cape Town light in mind when he named his book *True at First Light*, but we do know he was referring to Africa. This is the light that falls gently on the fishing boats when they take to the deep at dawn from the little harbour down the road to return with laden hulls around midday.

And if you wait patiently outside the harbour entrance, you might be able to bargain for a large, shiny fish directly from the trailer, which is handed over gutted and wrapped in newspaper.

From here it is a small hop to Giovanni's splendid deli and coffee bar in Main Road. The meeting place of all souls and the purveyor of food fit for the gods.

This is where I fill a basket with sweet vine tomatoes, glorious fresh basil, a creamy-centred buratta or two, walnut oil and balsamic vinegar, crusty bread, a wedge of Parmigiana and a brown paper bag filled with porcini mushrooms.

An armful of flowers, a quick glass of crispy white wine at the Slug and Lettuce next door and I'm ready for the short walk home through the neighbourhood's narrow lanes.

MUSIC FOR THIS CHAPTER: *Como paradis* by Christophe et Tony Raymond
OPPOSITE: *The early bird catches the worm. Oceana Powerboat Club, Mouille Point.*

- Rich duck soup
- Chicken stock
- Tagliolini with broccoli
- Cauliflower & avocado salad
- Leeks with walnut & truffle oil
- Lentil & chickpea salad with herbs
- Lamb with lemon & dill sauce
- Lamb pie
- Old-style venison batter
- Grilled cob with fennel & sauce vierge
- Ginger-poached pear & brandy tarts
- Fabulous fudge
- Pears in caramel sauce

Rich duck soup

Generous ladlesful of this fragrant soup are recommended during the soggy Cape winters.

Serves 8

- 1 duck
- 2 L chicken stock* (recipe opposite)
- 2 large onions
- 350 g carrots
- 3 leeks
- 1 stick celery with leaves
- 250 g potatoes, peeled
- 1 bouquet garni, made with sage, thyme, rosemary and bay leaves
- 2 T goose or duck fat
- 5 garlic cloves, peeled and chopped
- 3 T flat-leaf parsley, chopped
- 2 T flour
- salt and freshly ground black pepper

Rinse the duck and put it in a large soup pot. Cover with the stock. Bring it slowly to the boil, skim and simmer for about an hour. Chop the onions, carrots, leeks, celery and potatoes, and add to the soup with the bouquet garni. Simmer the soup slowly for at least another hour. Remove the duck from the pot, debone and shred the meat, skin and all, into bite-size pieces. Keep warm while you pour the soup through a sieve. Discard the bits, including the bouquet garni.

To thicken the soup you need to melt the goose or duck fat in a small saucepan. Add the garlic and parsley to the fat and braise gently before sprinkling the flour over the mixture. Stir until a thick paste forms. Slowly add a ladle of soup from the pot while you keep stirring the paste. Repeat until the mixture is thin enough before stirring it slowly into the soup. The soup will become really creamy.

Add the shredded meat to the soup and season to taste.

It is quite delicious served with a dollop of aioli** and a slice of crusty bread.

** See recipe on page 117.

A gourmet who thinks about calories is like a tart who looks at her watch.

JAMES BEARD

CHICKEN STOCK

- 1 free-range chicken
- 3 carrots, peeled and sliced into pennies
- 2 celery sticks with leaves, chopped
- 4 leeks, sliced into pennies and washed well
- 2 garlic cloves
- 1 bouquet garni, made with sage, thyme, parsley and a bay leaf
- 3 L water

Place all the ingredients in a large pot, cover with water and boil for about 2 hours. Pour through a sieve and discard the bits. Use the stock in soups.

Tagliolini with broccoli

Although I'm a staunch believer that starch is not necessarily the best food for a svelte figure, a little pasta is occasionally required to soothe the nerves. And this is a good dish to have up your sleeve.

Serves 6

- 500 g tagliolini pasta
- 600 g broccoli
- 250 ml extra virgin olive oil
- 12 anchovy fillets
- 4 cloves garlic, peeled and crushed
- 1 small chilli, pips discarded and chopped
- 1 handful flat-leaf parsley, chopped
- 50 g pine nuts, toasted

Break the broccoli from the stalk into tiny florets and boil them in a large pot of salted water until they are fairly well cooked but still crunchy. Drain them immediately and toss lightly with 25 ml of the extra virgin olive oil and a little salt. Keep warm.

Meanwhile, bring another large pot of well-salted water to the boil. Add the tagliolini and cook until the pasta is al dente.

While the pasta is cooking, place the rest of the olive oil, anchovies, garlic, chilli and the flat-leaf parsley in a large frying pan and fry gently over low heat. Stir to break up the anchovies. Take care not to burn the garlic.

When the tagliolini is cooked, drain the pasta, add the broccoli and toss it well with the anchovy mixture.

Garnish the pasta with a scattering of pine nuts and serve immediately in warmed bowls. Fabulous with a glass of Semillon.

LEFT: *Sea view from the harbour wall.*
ABOVE: *Fishing boat returning.*

ABOVE: *Flower stall next to Giovanni's.*

Cauliflower & avocado salad

This delightful salad goes particularly well with a gently braised fillet of white fish.

Serves 6

- 1 cauliflower
- 2 avocados, cubed
- 1 red pepper, chopped
- 75 ml black olives, chopped
- salt and pepper to taste
- 1 T capers, drained
- 1 T flour
- 1 T butter
- juice of 1 lemon
- 125 ml olive oil
- 1 T oregano, chopped
- 1 T chives, chopped

Steam the cauliflower very lightly, allow to cool and then break into florets and put in a salad bowl (if you prefer, leave the florets raw – it's crunchier that way). Add the avocado, red pepper and olives, toss together and season lightly.

Stir the capers and flour together, then scoop the capers out with a fork. Heat the butter in a pan and lightly sauté the flour-dusted capers in the hot butter. Sprinkle them over the salad.

Combine the lemon juice, olive oil and herbs, and spoon over the salad.

Serve with crusty bread.

ABOVE: *Wine for sale at the local deli.*

Leeks with walnut & truffle oil

This is a fabulously complementary dish to serve with a simply cooked fish fillet or chicken breast.

Serves 6

- 12 baby leeks
- 1 T extra virgin olive oil
- 60 ml walnut oil
- 20 ml truffle oil
- 1 t creamy French mustard
- 1 T fresh basil, chopped
- 1 T shallot, chopped
- 1 T tomato flesh, peeled and chopped
- 1 T diced courgette
- 1 T pine nuts, toasted

Discard the outside leaves of the baby leeks, cut the tips lengthwise and rinse the leeks really well. It helps to up-end them in a full jug of ice-cold water for a while. Cook in a saucepan of boiling water for no more than 5 minutes. Drain and gently pat dry.

Whisk the olive oil, walnut oil, truffle oil, mustard, basil and shallot together in a small bowl. Add the tomato, courgette and pine nuts and fold together.

Place the leeks on a warmed serving platter, spoon the vegetable and oil mixture over the leeks and serve immediately.

A good cook is like a sorceress who dispenses happiness. ELSA SCHIAPARELLI

Lentil & chickpea salad with herbs

A delicious winter salad to serve with a pan-fried fillet of fish. I always use dried lentils and chickpeas but the canned version would also be fine.

Serves 6

- 200 g lentils
- 200 g chickpeas, soaked overnight
- 2 carrots, chopped
- sea salt to taste
- 4 T walnut oil
- 1 T mild, creamy mustard
- 1 celery stalk, sliced into small bits
- 3 sprigs fresh coriander, chopped finely
- 10 sprigs chives, chopped finely
- 1 leek, chopped and rinsed well

Put the lentils and the chickpeas in boiling water with the chopped carrots, and cook for about 20 minutes. The pulses must still be firm but cooked. Season the vegetables with sea salt before adding the walnut oil and the mustard. Stir through gently.

Lightly toss together the finely chopped celery, coriander, chives and leeks. Add to the warm vegetables and mix gently.

Serve with a fillet of lightly pan-fried white fish.

TOP: *The 'local'.*
BELOW: *A treasure chest of vinegars and oils.*

Lamb with lemon & dill sauce

I love serving this on one of those endless summer days … when the young people come streaming through the front gate from Clifton beach, ravenous after a day playing beach volleyball and body surfing.

Serves 8

- 1.6 kg leg of deboned lamb, cubed
- 50 ml extra virgin olive oil
- 80 g spring onions, chopped
- 500 g baby spinach, washed
- 1 t dried fennel seeds
- 3 T dill, chopped
- 1 L chicken stock
- 3 egg yolks
- 175 ml lemon juice

ABOVE: *Deli fare.*

Heat the oil in a large saucepan and sauté the lamb for 10 minutes until it is gently browned. Add the spring onions, spinach, fennel seeds and dill. Add the chicken stock and simmer for about an hour or until the lamb is deliciously tender.

Use a ladle to spoon 200 ml of the broth from the stew into a jug.

Reduce the rest of the broth until it has reached a thick, sauce-like consistency. Spoon the tasty lamb stew onto a large serving platter and keep warm.

Put the egg yolks into a small bowl and whisk until pale and frothy. Slowly add the lemon juice while whisking vigorously. Pour a small amount of the broth into the yolks, whisking all the time. Add a little more and whisk. Keep whisking! Add the rest of the broth in a steady stream, constantly whisking … you really don't want this lot to curdle!

Transfer the mixture to a small saucepan and heat gently. Whisk while heating, until the mixture thickens enough to coat the back of a spoon. Do not boil.

Spoon the sauce over the lamb and serve immediately with rice.

Lamb pie

My friend, Eleanor, gave me a copy of a now delightfully dated cookbook that the Stellenbosch Fynproewersgilde had brought out. I still absolutely love this version of the recipe for venison pie which I later changed to a really saucy lamb pie. I use the original venison pie batter ... much as my grandmother, who grew up on a farm on the Polkadraai Road just outside Stellenbosch, used to do.
Serves 10 well

ABOVE AND LEFT: *An early morning peek at the harbour.*

- 1.5 kg lamb, preferably neck or stewing lamb
- 2 lamb shanks
- 100 ml extra virgin olive oil
- 1 T duck fat
- 750 ml dry white wine
- 1 carrot, peeled and sliced into pennies
- 4 leeks, sliced into pennies and washed well
- 1 celery stick with leaves, chopped
- 1 head of garlic, whole
- 10 cloves
- 1 T coriander seeds, ground in a mortar
- 6 juniper berries
- 3 bay leaves
- 1 t peppercorns
- 1 L chicken stock*
- salt and freshly ground black pepper

Preheat oven to 160 deg C/Gas 3.

In a large saucepan, heat the olive oil, melt the duck fat and braise the lamb and shanks until slightly browned. Add the wine and reduce by half over a fast, high heat. Add the carrot, leeks, celery, whole garlic, cloves, coriander, juniper berries, bay leaves and peppercorns. Pour the chicken stock into the saucepan to cover. Bring to the boil and cook until the meat is completely soft and falling from the bones.

I always use a slotted spoon to remove the meat from the saucepan. Allow the meat to cool down a little ... for obvious reasons! Debone the lamb carefully while shredding it with your fingers. Cover the meat and keep aside in a warm place. Pour the leftover stock through a sieve and return it to the saucepan. Reduce the stock until it has a sauce-like consistency. Spoon the hot sauce over the shredded meat. Mix gently. Season the meat with salt and freshly ground black pepper after tasting it. Butter a large ovenproof pie dish and transfer the saucy meat into the dish.

Spoon the creamy batter** carefully over the warm lamb and bake in the oven for 30 minutes or until the batter has risen slightly and turned a light caramel colour.

Serve the pie with a generous helping of cooked rice and some quince jelly on the side. Delicious!

* See recipe on page 71.
** See recipe on page 85.

Old-style venison batter

I love using this old-style batter for venison pies as well.

- 3 eggs, beaten
- 250 ml sunflower oil
- 250 ml milk
- 25 ml creamy mustard
- 240 g self-raising flour
- salt to taste

Beat the eggs, sunflower oil and milk well before adding the mustard. Fold the flour and the seasoning gently into the mixture.

Spoon over warm, shredded meat and bake.

RIGHT: *Fishing boats in the harbour.*
OPPOSITE PAGE: *The breakwater down the road.*

Grilled cob WITH FENNEL & SAUCE VIERGE

Living in Cape Town we certainly have a good choice of fresh fish. What a pleasure!

Serves 6

- 3 small fennel bulbs, sliced into pennies
- 4 T extra virgin olive oil
- 1 T butter
- 6 cob fillets
- 4 baby leeks, sliced into pennies and washed well
- 1 bunch dill, chopped
- 2 cloves garlic, chopped
- 50 g black olives, pitted and halved
- 4 tomatoes, peeled, seeded and chopped
- salt and freshly ground black pepper to taste

Fry the fennel very lightly in 2 T of the olive oil. Remove the fennel from the pan, melt a dollop of butter in the pan juices and fry the cob fillets on both sides until they are just done.

Remove the fillets from the pan and keep warm. Toss the fennel lightly in the pan juices and spoon over the fish fillets.

SAUCE VIERGE
To make the sauce vierge, roughly chop the leeks with the dill and the garlic. Add the halved olives and tomatoes and toss them all together in the rest of the olive oil. Taste the sauce vierge and season.

Serve the warm cob with the sauce vierge.

RIGHT: *Abundant shopping at Giovanni's.*

Ginger-poached pear & brandy tarts

An ideal dessert for winter. We should all know that almonds and pears were actually created for each other.

Serves 6

- 1 roll puff pastry, defrosted
- 120 g butter, softened
- 350 g castor sugar
- 200 g ground almonds
- 2 eggs
- 2 T brandy
- 5 ml vanilla paste
- 3 small pears, peeled
- 500 ml dry apple cider
- 1 finger ginger, peeled and sliced
- 1 star anise
- 125 g almonds, flaked and toasted
- thick cream to serve

Preheat the oven to 200 deg C/Gas 6.

Butter 6 small flan pans. Roll out the pastry and with a cutter slice 6 rounds in the pastry. Line the flan pans. Prick the dough with a fork and refrigerate.

To make the frangipane (almond cream), whisk the butter and 250 g of the castor sugar in a food processor until it is light and creamy. Add the ground almonds and eggs and mix well before adding the brandy and the vanilla paste. Scrape the creamy butter mixture into a bowl and refrigerate until needed.

In the meantime, poach the pears. Heat the cider and the remaining castor sugar in a small casserole dish with the ginger and star anise. Boil the pears in the sugary cider until they are tender. Remove the pears from the casserole dish and allow to cool a little. Cut each pear in half and remove the cores.

Pour the liquid through a sieve before returning it to the pan and reducing the remaining liquid until it has a syrupy consistency.

Remove the pastry cases and frangipane (almond cream) from the fridge and scoop a dollop of the frangipane into each pastry case. Place half a pear on top of each prepared pastry and bake for about 25 minutes or until the pastry is a lovely caramel colour.

Remove from the oven and garnish with a sprinkling of toasted almonds.

Serve with a healthy helping of thick cream. Fabulous!

ABOVE: *A quick cup of coffee at Giovanni's.*
OPPOSITE PAGE: *Served on a ceramic plate by Ruan Hoffman.*

Fabulous fudge

The biggest thrill was when my dad would venture into the kitchen and 'brew' some fudge. It still is actually! The recipe is from the little book Cook with Confidence, *published during 1956 in Cape Town by the Cape District Women's Auxiliary. The best fudge recipe ever!*

Makes quite enough

- 1.25 kg sugar
- 250 ml water
- 1 tin condensed milk
- 2 T butter
- 2 T golden syrup
- 1 t vanilla paste

Use a large pan and bring the sugar, water, condensed milk, butter and syrup to a slow boil. Keep boiling for about 45 minutes. You do not have to stir but you may if you want to! Add the vanilla paste and beat for 10 minutes in a food processor. Pour the fudge into a well-buttered pan and allow to cool partially before slicing it in small squares.

The best!

Pears in caramel sauce

The picture of a pear, oozing with caramel, resting in a wooden spoon, is possibly one of the more enchanting images I've ever seen. Here is a recreation of just that. And we all love the simplicity of a fruit for dessert, as well as the comfort of something deliciously sweet. Here you have both!

Serves 6

- 6 small ripe pears, peeled
- 250 ml white wine
- 125 ml brown sugar
- 250 ml cream
- 1 t vanilla paste

Heat the wine in a medium-sized pan, add the sugar and bring to a gentle simmer. Add the pears to the pan the moment all the sugar has dissolved. Poach until the pears are tender but still firm.

Remove the pears from the syrupy sauce, add the cream and the vanilla, and bring to a slow boil. Stir gently for about 5 minutes or until the sauce is gloriously thick.

Remove from the heat and stir the butter into the caramel sauce. Spoon the thick caramel over the pears and serve.

We cook from memories. We watched our mothers and our mothers' mothers, just as all the women in a family had watched and listened before them. Rather than learn how to cook, we inherit the way we cook and bake, like the colour of a father's eyes, the jut of a mother's chin. Like the past itself, which nourishes us at least as much as the food. And the rest is instinct …

AS QUOTED BY THE SENSUAL TOMASINA, FROM *THE LADY IN THE PALAZZO* BY MARLENA DE BLASI

Flavour me cinnamon

Sometimes the muted siren of the foghorn will call me from my bed for a slightly moody walk in the direction of the Mouille Point lighthouse. A walk which I know like the back of my hand, through what used to be the desolate Green Point common, and which is now the beautiful park that lies between home and the Atlantic. There, ducks have flown in to live in the freshwater lakes filled by ancient natural fountains; and tiny sugarbirds play among indigenous flora.

We'll have lunch at Mano's where, rumour has it, the lighting was changed to flatter the already luminous skins of the beautiful people who frequent this trendy bistro.

Just a short walk away is Anatoli's. I fondly recall the first time I had dinner there, about 20 years ago. We walked down the road from a friend's home in De Waterkant, carrying wine and a cluster of elegant long-stemmed crystal glasses, to be embraced by the rich patina of one of the most beautiful venues in Green Point. Greeted by the age-old Turkish ritual of a splendid tapas tray, followed by lamb and vegetable dishes redolent of far-away shores.

And naturally the slightly unsteady return up the hill.

Cherished memories.

MUSIC FOR THIS CHAPTER: *Bouton D'Or* by Viktor Lazlo
OPPOSITE: *Exotic kitchen at Anatoli's.*

- Rosalinda's spicy chicken soup

- Double-baked cheese soufflé

- Pasta in black olive cream

- Fennel, orange & walnut salad

- Ratatouille

- Delicious oven-roasted chicken

- Lamb & date tagine with couscous

- Rosemary-roasted pears

Rosalinda's spicy chicken soup

A delicious 'hot' soup that dropped into my mailbox from Rosalinda do Espirito Santo a couple of months ago. The most heart-warming of soups!

Serves 6

- 1.5 kg organic chicken
- 2 L home-made, rich chicken stock (page 71)
- 150 g spring onions, chopped
- 2 thumbs ginger, peeled and grated
- 4 red chillies, chopped
- 6 cloves garlic, chopped
- 4 T soy sauce
- 4 T lime juice, freshly squeezed
- 3 T brown sugar
- 200 g rice noodles
- handful fresh coriander leaves

Place the whole chicken in a large heavy-based saucepan and cover with the stock. Add the spring onions, ginger, chillies, garlic, soy sauce, lime juice and brown sugar to the stock and bring to a long rolling boil. Boil until the meat comes off easily from the bones.

Remove the chicken from the saucepan and debone carefully. I find that once the meat has cooled down a little it is actually easiest to do the deboning with your fingers. Shred the meat as you work.

Return the shredded meat to the saucepan and add the rice noodles. Cook until the noodles are al dente and serve the soup in warm soup bowls.

Garnish with a little fresh coriander and enjoy.

You only live once but if you
do it right, once is enough.

MAE WEST

ABUNDANCE

Double-baked cheese soufflé

I love serving this with a glass of really well-chilled, slightly wooded chardonnay.

Serves 6

- 60g butter
- 1 T flour
- 350 ml milk
- 250 g grated Gruyère cheese
- 1 T chives, chopped
- salt to taste
- 4 eggs, separated
- 500 ml pouring cream
- 1 T butter
- 2 T sage leaves

Preheat the oven to 180 deg C/Gas 4.

Melt the butter in a small saucepan, scoop the flour into the pan and stir until the mixture forms a doughy ball. Add the milk gradually and keep stirring until smooth and thick. Add 150 g of the Gruyère and combine. Remove the thick cheesy sauce from the heat and fold in the chives. Season to taste.

Add the egg yolks and mix well. In the meantime, whip the egg whites until firm peaks form. Fold the stiff egg whites into the cheesy mixture and spoon into 6 buttered and floured ramekin moulds.

Bake the soufflés in a bain-marie for about 30 minutes. Remove from the oven and allow to cool for about 10 minutes before you remove the moulds from the pan. (You do not want to burn yourself!) Run a small knife round the edges of the moulds and turn out onto small ovenproof serving dishes.

Pour a little cream over each soufflé, scatter the rest of the Gruyère over the soufflés and return to the oven for about 15 minutes.

In the meantime, heat the butter until it is a light brown colour. Quickly fry the sage leaves in the butter until they are crispy. Drain them on an absorbent sheet of paper. Remove the soufflés from the oven, garnish with the sage leaves and serve immediately.

*Cookery is
not chemistry.
It is an art.
It requires instinct and
taste rather than
exact measurements.*

MARCEL BOULESTIN

Pasta in black olive cream

The Green Point Park allows for a lovely walk through the most gorgeous fynbos … all the way from St George's Villa to the Green Point lighthouse. Once, when we arrived back home after one such meander, I threw some ingredients together and came up with this wonderfully easy dinner. Try this …

Serves 6

- 550 g tagliatelle pasta
- 300 g Parma ham, sliced
- 75 ml butter, diced
- 1 brown onion, peeled and chopped
- 3 garlic cloves, peeled and chopped
- 125 ml cream
- 75 g Gorgonzola
- 30 black olives, pitted and chopped
- salt and freshly ground black pepper

Heat the grill to medium and place the slices of Parma ham on a baking tray under the grill for about 10 minutes or until they are gloriously crisp. Remove from the oven and allow to cool down a little before gently cracking the Parma ham slices in little 4 cm shards. Keep aside.

Prepare the sauce by melting the butter and cooking the onion until transparent but not browned. Add the garlic. Add the cream and reduce the sauce until it is wonderfully thickened.

Turn down the heat and slowly stir the Gorgonzola into the cream sauce until it has completely melted. Make sure that the sauce does not come to the boil again.

Add the olives to the sauce.

In the meantime, cook the pasta in boiling salted water, drain, and quickly toss into the sauce.

Season to taste and serve immediately in warm pasta bowls, garnished with the shards of Parma ham.

ABOVE: *Interiors of Anatoli Turkish Restaurant in De Waterkant.*

Fennel, orange & walnut salad

We have really learned to appreciate walnuts since we spend some months of the year in Auvergne. This is a lovely autumn salad.

Serves 6

- 3 oranges, skin and pith removed
- 40 ml orange juice (reserved from segmenting oranges)
- 60 ml extra virgin olive oil
- 20 ml honey
- 1 t creamy mustard
- salt and freshly ground black pepper
- 3 fennel bulbs, sliced finely
- 150 g rocket leaves
- 60 g walnuts, chopped coarsely and toasted

Stand each orange upright and cut down the sides to remove all the skin as well as the pith. Hold each peeled orange in your hand over a bowl and cut down either side of each of the membranes to remove the segments. Drop them into the bowl and, when all the segments are removed, give the remnants of the oranges a good, solid squeeze to drain the rest of the juice.

Drain the orange segments and combine the orange juice with the olive oil, honey, mustard, salt and pepper to make the dressing.

Place the sliced fennel in a bowl, add dressing and toss well to coat.

Arrange the rocket on a serving platter or on individual plates and top with fennel and orange segments. Garnish the salad with the toasted walnuts and serve.

RIGHT: *Gentle scenes in Green Point Park.*

Ratatouille

The ultimate French vegetable dish. Delicious!

Serves 6

- 100 ml extra virgin olive oil
- 4 ripe red tomatoes, quartered
- 1 aubergine, diced roughly
- 4 courgettes, chopped roughly
- 1 red pepper, seeded and chopped roughly
- 1 green pepper, seeded and chopped roughly
- 2 onions, peeled and quartered
- 6 cloves garlic, halved
- salt and freshly ground black pepper to taste

Using a large cooking pot, heat the olive oil and add the tomatoes, aubergine, courgettes, peppers, onions and garlic. Place the lid firmly on top and steam gently until the vegetables release their fabulous aromatic juices. Then bring to a gentle boil, remove the lid and reduce the juices until the liquid reaches a thick, sauce-like consistency.

Taste and season carefully. The natural salt in the vegetables is normally quite enough.

Do not be tempted to stir! It will serve absolutely no purpose and you will only succeed in breaking up the vegetables.

Once the sauce is gloriously thick, spoon the ratatouille carefully into a serving dish with a large spatula, garnish with some freshly chopped parsley and serve.

Delicious oven-roasted chicken

Why is it that most of us still feel that this is the answer to all questions? A fabulous roast chicken with a slightly salty, crisp skin. Mmmm …

Serves 4

- 1 free-range chicken, whole
- 150 g Boursin®-style cheese with garlic and herbs
- 1 T extra virgin olive oil
- 1 T Maldon Salt
- 1 t paprika
- black pepper to taste

Preheat the oven to 180 deg C/Gas 4.

With a sharp knife, remove the tiny glands in the 'pope's nose' before gently working all the creamy cheese underneath the skin over the breast of the chicken. Use a small sharp knife to lift the skin and your fingers to do the cheese bit.

Place the chicken into an ovenproof casserole dish, baste with the olive oil and rub with the salt, paprika and pepper.

Cook covered in the oven for 1 hour, basting the chicken regularly. Cut the chicken into portions and dress it with the cooking juices.

I normally serve this with a green salad and a piece of crusty bread.

ABOVE: *The lighthouse spotted from the Green Point Park.*

MIDDLE AND BOTTOM: *Walking and jogging in Green Point Park.*

ABUNDANCE

Lamb & date tagine WITH COUSCOUS

I just love the dusty notes that are created with the generous use of Moroccan spices. This lamb and date tagine is no exception.

Serves 10

- 2.5 kg stewing lamb
- 3 T extra virgin olive oil
- 3 T butter
- 2 cardamom pods, shelled
- 2 t paprika
- 1 t dried ginger
- 1 T cumin
- 1 T ground coriander
- 2 cinnamon sticks
- 1 head of garlic
- 2 bay leaves
- 20 whole dates, pitted
- 125 g pine nuts, roasted

COUSCOUS

- 500 g couscous
- salt and freshly ground black pepper to taste
- 1 t saffron
- 1 T extra virgin olive oil
- 3 red peppers, peeled, seeded and chopped
- 250 g black olives, pitted

Heat the oil and butter in a large saucepan and brown the meat well. Add the cardamom, paprika, ginger, cumin, coriander and cinnamon to the meat. Cover with water and bring to a gentle rolling boil. Add the garlic and bay leaves. Allow the stew to simmer for about 1 hour. Add more water if it seems necessary. Reduce the liquid until it has a thick, sauce-like consistency. Add the dates and braise for at least another 10 minutes or until the meat is completely succulent. You can add a little water if necessary. Spoon the lamb onto a large platter and garnish with the pine nuts.

In the meantime, season the dry couscous and steam it with boiling water to which you have added the saffron. The water should just cover the couscous.

In a small pan, heat the olive oil and quickly stir the red pepper and black olives through the oil. Spoon the warm mixture onto the steaming couscous before serving it with the juicy lamb.

TOP: *Water wheel in the Green Point Park.*
BELOW: *View of Green Point Stadium from the park.*

Rosemary-roasted pears

There are so many ways to skin a pear ... and I love them all.

Serves 6

- 3 firm, ripe pears, peeled, halved and cored
- 30 g unsalted butter, melted
- 6 good sprigs rosemary
- 50 g castor sugar
- 3 star anise
- 250 g ripened Brie

Preheat the oven to 200 deg C/Gas 6.

Rub the pear halves with the butter. Place the pear halves on top of the rosemary sprigs in a buttered roasting pan and sprinkle with the sugar. Add the star anise to the pan. Roast in the oven for 20–25 minutes or until the pears are tender and glazed.

Carefully cut the ripened Brie into 6 slices and place with a pear half on individual plates. Garnish with a small sprig of rosemary.

FAR LEFT: *Lion's Head from the Green Point Park.*
MIDDLE: *Mouille Point lighthouse.*
ABOVE: *The favourite fashion café, Mano's.*

News: Haas Collective was voted "Top 20 Reasons to be in SA"
— *Wallpaper Magazine Nov 20

chapter 6

Coffee & thyme

Cobbled and cosmopolitan streets haunted by the call to prayer from ancient mosques, party people recovering over buttery eggs on shady bistro pavements. The noon gun's muffled boom, the rich aroma of roasting coffee beans. Narrow lanes and gloriously colourful cottages with deep purple and lilac bougainvillea climbing the walls. This is the vibrant cultural melting pot where De Waterkant – also known as the Pink Village – meets the traditional Muslim community of the Bo Kaap.

Tiny shops spill exquisite objets, from Panama hats to the sweetest of cakes, beautifully woven carpets and a tiny sculpture that is just so. This is the insiders' meeting spot: from the fabulous La Petite Tarte to the trendy coffee experience at Origin; the slave museum coffee shop Truth, where the laptop brigade seek inspiration and wireless connections, to the designer shop and bistro Loading Bay.

Stop for lunch with the ever-generous Marco at Marco's African Place for a plateful of wholesome food.

And then you travel up the aptly named Rose Street towards the little shop Haas and its adjacent bistro where, en route from the city after a day's work, you see the beau monde relaxing with a glass of chilled wine.

This is the ancient heart of this glorious city beating strong.

MUSIC FOR THIS CHAPTER: *Manha De Carnival* by Jim Tomlinson
OPPOSITE: *Haas in Rose Street.*

- Bourride

- Aioli

- Anchovy bruschetta

- Jarvis Street fasolia

- Tomato tarts with pesto

- Potato salad with egg & aioli

- Barbecued leg of lamb

- Short ribs in raisin sauce

- Figs with pistachio frangipane

Bourride

This rich fish soup can be served in a variety of ways. The broth may be served with croutons and the fish eaten separately with boiled potatoes as a main course. I adore spooning huge dollops of aioli on top as well! Or serving it with a small slice of anchovy bruschetta on the side …

Serves 6

GARLIC CROUTONS

- ½ stale baguette, sliced
- 60 ml olive oil
- 10 garlic cloves, ground to a smooth paste
- salt and black pepper to taste

STOCK

- ¼ t saffron threads
- 1 T water
- 1 L dry white wine
- 3 leeks, chopped
- 1 fennel bulb, chopped
- 2 carrots, peeled and chopped
- 2 long pieces orange zest
- 2 teaspoons fennel seeds
- 3 sprigs thyme
- some fish bones, heads and trimmings
- 3 egg yolks
- salt and black pepper to taste

FISH

- 2.5 kg whole firm white fish, such as monkfish, angelfish, cob, sole or even red roman, filleted, skinned and cut into 4 cm pieces
- butter
- extra virgin olive oil

To make the croutons, preheat the oven to 160 deg C/Gas 2–3. Brush the bread with oil and bake for 10 minutes until crisp. Put lashings of garlic on one side of each slice of toast. Season with salt and pepper.

For the stock, soak the saffron in a tablespoon of hot water for 15 minutes. Put the saffron, wine, leeks, fennel, carrots, orange zest, fennel seeds, thyme and all the fish bits and trimmings into a large saucepan with 3 litres of water. Cover and bring to the boil, then simmer for 1 hour, skimming occasionally. Strain into a clean saucepan, pressing the solids with a wooden spoon to extract all the liquid.

While the stock is simmering, cook the fish. In a pan, melt the butter in the olive oil and toss the pieces of fish gently in the pan until they are lightly cooked. Remove from the pan and keep warm. Season with salt and pepper to taste. Return the stock to the saucepan and bring the liquid to a gentle simmer. Boil for 5 minutes, or until slightly reduced, and remove from the heat.

Put the egg yolks in a bowl. Whisk in a ladleful of hot stock and gradually add 4 ladlesful, whisking constantly. Repeat the process until the egg yolks are perfectly amalgamated with the stock. Pour the egg mixture back into the pan and whisk over low heat for 3–5 minutes, or until the soup is hot and slightly thicker (don't let it boil or it will curdle). Season with salt and pepper.

To serve, place a few pieces of fish in a soup bowl, spoon the rich soup over the fish, top with the garlic croutons and serve. I also, on occasion, serve this delicious soup with aioli and garlic and anchovy croutons on the side.

Garlic is as good as ten mothers.

LES BLANK

ABOVE: *Conrad Hicks sculpture.*
RIGHT: *Cover against the sun.*

Aioli

I serve this in large dollops with the bourride.

Serves 6

- 8 cloves garlic, peeled
- a little salt
- 3 egg yolks
- 300 ml olive oil
- 1 t smooth mustard

Pound the garlic and a little salt with a mortar and pestle until it forms a smooth paste. Then add the egg yolks and whisk. Scrape the mixture into a food processor and, with the motor running, add the olive oil in a thin, steady stream until the mixture forms a smooth and creamy mayonnaise.

ABOVE: *Counter top in La Petite Tarte.*
RIGHT: *Interiors shop in Jarvis Street.*

Anchovy bruschetta

This is another option to serve with bourride. I often serve this as a snack with a glass of white wine.

Serves 6

- 6 slices rustic bread
- 1 clove garlic, peeled
- 60 ml extra virgin olive oil
- 12 salted anchovies

Grill the bread lightly. Then rub the top side with the garlic clove, dip both sides in the olive oil and top with the anchovy fillets.

ABOVE: *Street scenes in De Waterkant.*

Jarvis Street fasolia

My De Waterkant friend, Heather, regularly serves this with some bread before dinner. Sooo good!

Serves 6

- 300 g mixed dried pulses, * soaked overnight
- 1 large brown onion, peeled and chopped
- 200 ml extra virgin olive oil
- 4 cloves garlic, peeled and crushed
- 1 T fresh thyme, chopped finely
- 1 red chilli, seeded and chopped
- 2 very ripe tomatoes, peeled and chopped
- juice of 2 lemons
- salt and freshly ground pepper

Fry the onion lightly in the olive oil in a deep saucepan until it is perfectly glossy but not browned. Strain the pulses and add to the onion with the garlic, thyme, chilli and tomatoes. Give it one good stir then allow it to simmer away peacefully in its own juices for about 10 minutes. Cover with boiling water and keep simmering over a gentle heat for about 2 hours.

Add the lemon juice and season to taste.

Scoop into a lovely bowl or six small bowls and serve with crispy bread.

* I like using chickpeas, lentils, kidney beans and even some sugar beans.

OPPOSITE TOP: *Lunch at Loading Bay.*
OPPOSITE BOTTOM: *Shopfront in Jarvis Street.*
ABOVE: *Cluster of Vespas in Rose Street.*

*Food is the fulfilment of fertile earth, gentle seasons,
the crucible of the sun and heavenly rain.*

JOHN JACKSON

Tomato tarts with pesto

This is a delicious little starter to indulge in. I've recently been given armfuls of freshly cut basil … hence the tarts!

Serves 6

- 1 roll puff pastry, defrosted
- 125 g freshly grated Parmesan
- 125 g grated Gruyère
- 150 g feta, crumbled
- 125 g cherry tomatoes, sliced
- freshly made basil pesto*

Preheat the oven to 200 deg C/Gas 6, then butter 6 small, loose-bottomed tart pans well.

Line each pan with the thawed, lightly rolled out puff pastry and pre-bake for about 10 minutes.

Lightly mix the Parmesan, Gruyère and feta together. Fill each pastry case with the cheese mixture and arrange the cherry tomato slices on top. Return to the oven for about 10 minutes.

In the meantime, make the creamy basil pesto.* Remove the tarts from the oven, spoon a dollop of pesto on top and serve immediately with a small salad.

* See recipe on page 171.

FROM LEFT TO RIGHT: *Haas interior. Front door in De Waterkant. Manhattens. Menus at La Petite Tarte.*

Potato salad with egg & aioli

This is a really good salad that you can prepare quite a bit before your guests arrive. It's always better if the flavours have time to 'marry' a little.

Serves 6

- 8 medium potatoes, washed and boiled in salted water until soft
- 6 eggs, boiled over medium heat, peeled and coarsely chopped
- 1 T small capers
- 2 T cocktail gherkins, chopped
- 125 g spring onions, chopped finely
- salt and white pepper
- 400 ml aioli*

Drain the cooked potatoes, and peel them once they have cooled down a bit. Slice the potatoes into 3 cm pieces and drop them into a large salad bowl. Add the eggs, capers, gherkins and the chopped spring onions. Season well and toss the creamy aioli through the salad.

Cover the salad and keep in a cool place. Serve after about 3 hours … it will be delicious!

* See recipe on page 117.

ABOVE: *Coffee at Origin in Hudson Street.*

Barbecued leg of lamb

It is not too tricky to debone and butterfly a leg of lamb. Just slice straight to the bone dividing the meat in two. Using a small sharp knife you can then gently carve the bone out of the meat. Easy!

Serves 8

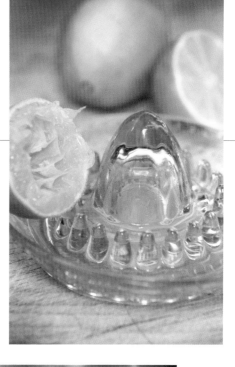

- 1.5 kg leg of lamb, butterflied
- 6 cloves garlic, peeled and chopped finely
- 3 T thyme, chopped
- 3 T parsley, chopped
- 3 t oregano, chopped
- 2 T extra virgin olive oil
- freshly squeezed juice of 2 limes
- salt and freshly ground black pepper to taste

Light your fire!

Mix the garlic, thyme, parsley and oregano with the olive oil and lime juice in a small bowl. Season the herb mixture to taste.

Place the butterflied leg of lamb into a large dish and cut shallow slits into the meat.

Using your fingers, rub the herb mixture thoroughly into the meat.

Allow the meat to 'soak' up the herbs for at least an hour while you wait for the coals to be ready. Once you feel safe with the heat, barbecue the meat until it is cooked. This should take about 45 minutes over moderate coals.

Slice thinly and serve with boiled baby potatoes.

The conviviality around the table has as much to do with the people around it as the food upon it.

PETE GOFFE-WOOD

RIGHT: *Freshly laid limes!*

Short ribs in raisin sauce

My father fed us short ribs in raisin sauce every day for a week while my mother was in hospital 'fetching' my baby sister. I never ate it again – until recently when I was asked to do a TV show on family recipes, and found that it is actually lovely!

Serves 8

- 75 ml extra virgin olive oil
- 1 T butter
- 1.4 kg beef short ribs
- salt and black pepper to taste
- 1 onion, chopped
- 1 t creamy mustard
- 2 T lemon juice
- 1 bay leaf
- 125 g raisins
- 125 g brown sugar
- 1 t grated lemon rind
- 500 ml beef stock

Warm the olive oil and butter in a large casserole dish.

Cut the short ribs into comfortable pieces. Season with salt and pepper, and brown in the casserole dish.

Add the onion and sauté with the ribs until the onions are translucent. Add the rest of the ingredients and bring to the boil (add water if it looks like it needs a little more liquid).

Simmer for about 2 hours or until the meat is tender and the sauce is beautifully reduced and quite sticky.

Serve with baby potatoes or wild rice.

RIGHT: *Haas, Rose Street in the Bo Kaap.*
FAR RIGHT: *Pensive girl.*

ABOVE: *Attendance register at Origin.*

Figs with pistachio frangipane

Early autumn in the Cape is always fig time. We buy them beautifully stacked in boxes at our local deli.
What an indulgence.

Serves 8

- 8 ripe figs, whole
- 150 g pistachio nuts
- 60 g unsalted butter, soft
- 1 T castor sugar
- 1 egg, beaten
- 2 T cake flour
- 1 T Grand Marnier liqueur

ZESTY SYRUP
- 250 ml white wine
- 150 g castor sugar
- zest of one orange
- 2 cinnamon sticks
- 3 cloves
- 1 t black peppercorns, whole
- fresh basil

Heat the oven to 180 deg/Gas 4.

Grind the pistachio nuts with a pestle and mortar until they have a floury consistency. Cream the butter and sugar together and add the egg. Whisk well before adding the ground pistachio nuts and the flour. Add the Grand Marnier and fold in well.

Break the figs open in halves and spoon a dollop of the frangipane into each. Place the filled fig halves in a buttered ovenproof dish and bake in the warm oven for about 8 minutes.

Pour the wine into a medium-sized pan and bring to a slow boil. Add the sugar, orange zest, cinnamon sticks, cloves and peppercorns. Dissolve the sugar and reduce the spicy wine to syrup.

Remove from the heat and spoon over the still-warm figs.

Serve with a fresh basil leaf.

chapter 7

Fork on Long

*T*ake a walk from the top of the mid-seventeenth century Company Gardens in front of the imposing gates of the Mount Nelson Hotel, pass the Iziko Art Museum, and follow the tree-lined avenue towards the centre of the city. Take a detour to the rose gardens that were established in 1929.

Swing to the left and skip down Bree Street for an early morning snack and an excellent cappuccino at Jason Bakery.

Trundle down, then, to Long Street, and take note of Minato, where you will find arguably the best sushi in the Cape. Further along is the Pan African Market with its jewel-coloured balcony, and the delectable tapas at Fork. Or perhaps you feel more like the colonial Maremoto, vegetarian Zucchini, or the trendy Royale Eatery for a splendid hamburger?

Do stop at Clarke's Bookshop. Spend time among long-forgotten writers and famous authors. Turn the yellowed pages carefully and read quietly in the dusky light.

Amble in the direction of Greenmarket Square and hover for a moment under the trees of Café Mozart in Church Street.

And tonight, don a piece from your 'downtown New York' wardrobe and book a table at Societi Bistro in Orange Street.

You are breathing the city.

MUSIC FOR THIS CHAPTER: *Cockeyed Optimist* by Jim Tomlinson and Stacey Kent
OPPOSITE: *The night is young. Long Streeet early evening.*

- Baked egg with cream cheese

- Tuna pâte rolled in puff pastry

- Mushroom tart

- Red pepper, tomato & chickpea salad

- Roasted butternut & sage

- Pan-fried white fish with sage leaves & artichoke hearts

- Whole pork knuckles with white wine & garlic

- Carrot cake with creamy icing

Baked egg with cream cheese

This is a delicious way of serving an English breakfast with a twist.

Serves 6

- 600 ml pouring cream
- 6 eggs
- 100 g bacon, finely chopped and fried in butter
- 30 g cream cheese
- butter
- salt and pepper

Preheat the oven to 200 deg C/Gas 6.

Season the cream lightly with salt and pepper.

Butter six individual ramekins. Crack an egg into each one, taking care not to break the yolk, and add a teaspoon of bacon and some cream cheese. Spoon the cream into the ramekins, making sure that you just cover the eggs.

Bake in a bain-marie for about 10 minutes.

Serve with a thin finger of toast.

RIGHT: *The colonial-looking Maremoto on Long.*

Tuna pâté rolled in puff pastry

This is one of the old family regulars that is often served as a light lunch during boisterous holidays!

Serves 8

- 1 roll puff pastry, defrosted
- 1 tin flaked tuna in oil, drained
- 2 eggs, hardboiled and grated finely
- 1 onion, chopped finely
- 1 clove garlic, chopped
- 3 T mayonnaise
- 2 T parsley, chopped
- salt and pepper to taste

Preheat the oven to 200 deg C/Gas 6.

In a large mixing bowl and using a fork, mix the tuna, eggs, onion, garlic and mayonnaise together until the mixture has an almost rough pâté consistency. Add the parsley and season to taste.

Unroll the puff pastry and spoon the pâté on top of it. Using a fork, spread the filling across the pastry until it is completely covered. Gently fold the pastry into a roll lengthwise.

With a sharp knife, slice the roll into 5cm-thick wheels. Place these on a buttered baking tray and bake for about 20 minutes or until the pastry is completely cooked and crispy with a delicious caramel colour.

Serve the tuna wheels with a fresh garden salad with lots of avocado. Wonderful, easy food!

OPPOSITE: *Long Street Swimming Pool.*
ABOVE LEFT: *Street food on Long.*
ABOVE RIGHT: *Hamburgers at Royale Eatery.*

Remember that a very good sardine is always preferable to a not so good lobster.

FERRAN ADRIA

Mushroom tart

Autumn in the Cape means gentle early morning forays into a misty forest looking for that secret sprouting of mushrooms. And what a pleasure it is to brush the dark soil from your pickings while planning your menu …

Serves 6

- 20 whole fresh button mushrooms, thinly sliced
- 50 g butter
- extra virgin olive oil
- 1 leek, finely chopped
- 100 g smoked chicken, shredded
- 50 g bacon bits
- 150 ml pouring cream
- 2 cloves garlic
- 1 egg, beaten
- 1 roll flaky pastry
- sea salt and freshly ground black pepper

LEFT: *Café Mozart.*
ABOVE: *The well-loved Jason Bakery on Bree.*

Heat the oven to 200 deg C/Gas 6.

Melt the butter in a very hot pan and sauté the thinly sliced mushrooms until they have a lovely nutty colour, smell and taste.

Heat the olive oil and gently braise the leek, smoked chicken and bacon. Add the cream and reduce to a sauce-like consistency. Add the garlic. Allow the mixture to cool for about 20 minutes. Fold in the egg.

Roll out the pastry, cover it completely with the creamy mixture and arrange the mushrooms on top.

Season lightly and bake for about 20 minutes or until the pastry is well-baked and a light caramel colour.

Serve with a small green salad.

ABOVE: *Fingerposts to pleasure.*

Red pepper, tomato & chickpea salad

One of the most deliciously beautiful dishes I have ever put together … and surprisingly healthy as well!

Serves 8

- 6 red peppers, peeled and quartered
- 1 red chilli, seeded and chopped
- handful flat-leaf parsley, chopped
- 650 g chickpeas, cooked
- 350 g baby tomatoes
- 125 ml olive oil
- 4 cloves garlic, chopped
- 200 g chèvre (goat's milk cheese)
- salt and black pepper to taste

Toss the red pepper and the chilli with the flat-leaf parsley. Spoon the chickpeas onto a large serving platter. Layer the red pepper mixture on top of the chickpeas.

In the meantime, place the tomatoes in a small casserole dish, pour the olive oil over them and braise over a high heat until the tomatoes have popped their skins and the juices have amalgamated with the oil to make a light tomato sauce. Add the chopped garlic and cook for another 3 minutes. Take care not to burn the garlic.

Remove from the heat. Spoon the warm tomato and olive oil dressing over the chickpeas and red pepper salad. Tear the soft, ripe chèvre apart with your fingers and drop the pieces into the warm topping. Season to taste.

Serve immediately.

RIGHT: *Skinny Legs & All on Loop Street.*

ABOVE: *Fountain in Company Gardens.*
RIGHT: *Walking down The Avenue from the Mount Nelson Hotel.*

ABUNDANCE

FROM TOP LEFT CLOCKWISE: *Houses of Parliament; Entrance to church on Greenmarket Square; Greenmarket Square; Restaurant at the Pan African Market;*
Mask seller at Pan African Market; Slave bell – Company Gardens; Iziko Art Museum.

ABOVE: *Societi Bistro.*

Roasted butternut & sage

This is always a wonderful accompaniment to a pork or venison dish. And how I do love the slightly dusty flavour of fresh sage!

Serves 8

- 2 whole butternut, quartered, pips removed, skin on
- 20 ml olive oil
- 50 ml boiling hot water
- 50 g butter
- handful fresh sage leaves
- salt and freshly ground black pepper

Preheat the oven to 180 deg C/Gas 4.

Place the butternut quarters, skin down, in an ovenproof dish. Brush every piece with a little olive oil. Add the water to the pan to just cover the base. Cover with foil and steam/bake the butternut for about 5 minutes. Remove the foil and roast for another 20 minutes.

Melt the butter in a very warm saucepan and quick-fry the sage leaves until they are quite crisp.

Remove the butternut slices from the oven. Spoon a couple of the crisped sage leaves and butter over the butternut slices, season to taste and serve.

'Tis an ill cook that cannot lick his own fingers.

WILLIAM SHAKESPEARE

ABOVE: *Chefs behind the hot pass at Societi Bistro.*
RIGHT: *Diners at Societi Bistro.*

Pan-fried white fish WITH SAGE LEAVES & ARTICHOKE HEARTS

This is utterly delicious served with a good dab of dill or fennel butter.

Serves 6

- 850 g white fish such as cob, hake or angelfish, skinned and boned and filleted
- 15 ml extra virgin olive oil
- 10 ml butter
- handful sage leaves
- 24 asparagus spears, washed
- 6 artichoke hearts, sliced*
- salt and freshly ground black pepper to taste

Preheat the oven to 220 deg C/Gas 7.

Slice the fish in portions. In a pan, heat the oil and butter together, and fry the fish with the sage leaves until the fish is just taking colour. Place in a hot oven for 3 minutes or so to cook through, depending on the thickness of the fish fillets.

Just before serving, reheat the pan juices and add the asparagus with the artichoke hearts, season to taste, toss gently and remove from the heat. Place the asparagus and artichoke hearts in the middle of each individual plate. Place a slice of fish on top of the vegetables and spoon the dill butter on top. Garnish with fresh dill and serve immediately.

* I don't hesitate to use preserved artichoke hearts if I can't find lovely fresh ones.

DILL BUTTER

- 500 g butter
- 125 g fresh dill, chopped (or, if you feel like it, substitute the same volume of chopped fennel leaves)
- 25 ml fish sauce
- juice of 1 lemon
- 2 pinches salt
- 2 pinches white pepper
- 2 t Dijon mustard
- 2 t cream

Gently melt the butter, add the dill and bring to a gentle simmer. Add the rest of the ingredients and check seasoning. Whisk thoroughly and keep warm; whisk again just before serving.

If you have to ask what jazz is,
you'll never understand.

LOUIS ARMSTRONG

TOP: *Alfresco lunch at Jason Bakery.*
ABOVE: *Be warned!*

Whole pork knuckles with white wine & garlic

There is always genuine pleasure in putting these fragrant ingredients together in my huge blue casserole dish. And taking it from the stove straight to the table where all our friends just help themselves. I always have a heap of pan-fried new potatoes on the side to mop up the sauce.

Serves 6

- 1.5 kg pork knuckles
- 50 ml extra virgin olive oil
- 1 T butter
- 500 ml dry white wine
- 2 T marjoram, chopped
- 2 T thyme, chopped
- 2 T sage, chopped
- 4 cloves
- 2 star anise
- 6 cloves garlic, peeled and chopped
- 1 L chicken stock
- salt and freshly ground black pepper to taste

Heat the olive oil in a large … preferably blue … casserole dish. Melt the butter in the olive oil before adding the knuckles. Brown the meat well before pouring in the wine. Bring the wine to a rolling boil and allow all the alcohol to evaporate before adding the marjoram, thyme, sage, cloves, star anise and garlic. Add the chicken stock and bring to a gentle simmer.

Cook for about an hour or until the meat is absolutely tender and the cooking liquid has reduced to a lovely thick sauce consistency.

Place the blue casserole dish in the middle of the table and enjoy!

RIGHT AND MIDDLE: *Best loved tapas in town.*
FAR RIGHT: *The author having a well-deserved lunch at Fork.*

Carrot cake with creamy icing

I've always wanted to bake a really moist, spicy carrot cake with at least an extra inch of wonderfully rich creamy cheese icing on top. The topping is always the best part of a cake, methinks. This is definitely it.

Serves 10

- 250 g self-raising cake flour
- 2 t ground cinnamon
- 1 t nutmeg, grated
- 1 t allspice
- ¼ t salt
- 200 g light muscovado sugar
- 3 eggs
- 150 ml vegetable oil
- 75 ml milk
- 1 t vanilla paste
- 250 g carrots, peeled and grated finely
- 100 g shredded tinned pineapple, drained
- 125 g walnuts, chopped

CREAM CHEESE ICING

- 500 g smooth cream cheese
- 250 g crème fraîche
- 150 g icing sugar, sifted
- 2 t vanilla paste

Preheat the oven to 180 deg C/Gas 4.

Butter and flour a cake tin of your choice.

In a medium bowl, sift together the flour, cinnamon, nutmeg, allspice and salt. In a large bowl or food processor, mix the sugar and eggs until the mixture is all foamy. At low speed, add the vegetable oil before folding the dry, sifted ingredients into the egg mixture. Fold in the milk as well as the vanilla paste. Spoon the carrots, pineapple and walnuts into the dough and fold through carefully.

Transfer the mixture into the greased cake tin and bake in the middle of the heated oven for about 50 minutes or until a skewer comes out clean. Remove the cake from the oven and let it cool in the pan for at least 15 minutes before turning it out onto a wire cake rack.

CREAM CHEESE ICING

In a medium bowl, fold the cream cheese, crème fraîche and icing sugar together until the mixture is completely smooth and absolutely creamy. Fold the vanilla paste into the mixture.

Move the cooled cake to a lovely cake stand and spoon the cheese icing on top, spreading it roughly with the back of the spoon.

Serve large slices immediately!

chapter 8

Street of gold

*O*n a warm and balmy African evening, sometimes, the call of our dark continent is compelling. Walk down the worn steps of Martin Melck House on Strand Street and into the walled courtyard that houses the Gold Restaurant. The expectation that fills the air soon turns to wonderment at the richness of our heritage. Warm colours and ancient sounds. Glorious puppets and majestic masks. The African tapas, the vibrant dancers and the songs that are the essence of Africa ring true here.

If you slip through the little door at the back of the courtyard, you will be just behind Hemelhuijs, a bistro that not only changes its menu every season but – like a chameleon – also its colour. Heavenly, fun food. The chef might hand you a jar of pickles from his mother as a gift, or linger at your table to enjoy a glass of wine.

Across the paved road, between two rustic buildings, nestles the Peruvian eatery Keenwä. Here we start our meal with a pisco, and follow through with a fresh and tart ceviche and quinoa with chillies. It's transportation to another world.

And if you are in the know, you'll find your way to Bizerca Bistro for the most splendid French plate of food down town. You'll want to weep with joy at the tasty morsels.

And that is what living in this wonderful, wise city is all about.

MUSIC FOR THIS CHAPTER: *Explode Coração* by Maria Bethânia
OPPOSITE: *Dancers and puppets at the Gold Museum.*

- Rustic mushroom soup

- Pork rashers with potatoes & goat's cheese on rye

- Buffalo mozzarella salad with fennel & caperberries

- Creamy veal stew

- Chicken with sherry & cream

- Pork chops with port

- Quince crumble

Rustic mushroom soup

As always, in times of distress, one should be able to resort to a nourishing mushroom soup.

Serves 6

- 150 g smoked bacon, chopped finely
- 4 leeks, chopped finely and washed well
- 5 T extra virgin olive oil
- 1 T duck fat
- 100 g butter
- 750 g wild or brown mushrooms, wiped clean and sliced
- 2 L rich chicken stock*
- 125 ml thick cream
- sea salt and freshly ground black pepper
- nutmeg, freshly ground

Cook the bacon in a large, dry saucepan over medium heat until the fat begins to run. Tip in the leeks and continue cooking until they are soft but not discoloured. Add the olive oil and duck fat to the pan and simmer gently over a low heat while you melt the butter in another pan. Brown the butter completely before adding the mushrooms to it. Once the mushrooms are beautifully caramelised, add them to the leek mixture and cook together for about 4 minutes. Add the rich chicken stock and bring to a rolling boil for about 20 minutes.

To complete the soup, add in the cream. Stir carefully to combine, and warm gently for a further minute until piping hot. Do not boil. Season with salt and pepper, and spoon the soup into warm bowls.

Garnish with a little nutmeg and serve with crusty bread.

* See recipe on page 71.

Pork rashers with potatoes & goat's cheese ON RYE

I stole this recipe without any guilt from one of the most appetising pictures of sumptuous food I have ever seen. I only had the photograph as guidance ... all guesswork really!

Serves 6

- 6 fresh pork rashers, cut thickly and sliced into bite-sized bits
- 200 ml extra virgin olive oil
- 12 new potatoes, roasted in the skin
- 1 head of garlic, roasted whole and peeled
- 6 sprigs rosemary, leaves stripped from the stems and chopped
- 6 slices rye bread, toasted
- 300 g soft goat's milk cheese, sliced into rounds
- salt and freshly ground pepper to taste
- green peppercorns, to serve
- 4 red chillies, chopped

Heat 100 ml of the olive oil in a saucepan and fry the pork bites in the oil until they are fabulously golden brown and cooked. Remove the pork from the pan and keep warm. Quarter the roasted potatoes and add them, as well as the peeled garlic, to the pan for a quick stir in the olive oil. Turn off the heat and spoon the pork rashers back into the pan. Add the rosemary. Toss the mixture lightly together.

Place the toasted slices of rye bread onto individual plates and spoon the warm pork and potato on top of the bread.

Add the slices of goat's milk cheese and season to taste. Serve with a little pot of green peppercorns and a small jug with the rest of the olive oil to sprinkle over this delicious concoction.

ABOVE RIGHT: *African Queen dusting gold.*
RIGHT: *Dancing with puppets at Gold.*
FAR RIGHT: *Marimba playing at Gold Restaurant.*

Buffalo mozzarella salad WITH FENNEL & CAPERBERRIES

I invented this salad one Sunday lunchtime when I realised I'd better pull something special out of the hat for a couple of gourmand friends. It was lovely!

Serves 6

- fresh rocket, one portion per person
- 3 baby fennel bulbs, sliced thinly
- 2 T extra virgin olive oil
- salt and pepper to taste
- 2 fresh, whole buffalo mozzarella rounds, sliced
- 1 T caperberries, drained
- 1 T flour
- 1 T butter
- handful fresh sage leaves
- 6 anchovies

Cover a large serving platter* with the rocket. Toss the sliced fennel with one tablespoon of the olive oil, season lightly and scatter over the rocket. Top with the mozzarella slices.

Stir the caperberries and flour together, then scoop the caperberries out with a fork. Heat the butter in a pan and frizzle the flour-dusted caperberries in the hot butter until crisp. Remove and scatter over the salad.

Add the rest of the olive oil to the pan and reheat. When the oil is smoking, add the sage leaves to the pan. Remove from the heat immediately, and spoon the crisp sage and buttery sauce over the salad.

Garnish with the anchovies and serve as a starter, or as a salad with fish.

* You could also prepare the salad on individual plates for a more formal starter.

RIGHT: *Golden Africa moments.*

Creamy veal stew

This stew, or blanquette de veau, *is one of those dishes I really think we should prepare a little more often. Satisfying and utterly comforting!*

Serves 8

- 1.5 kg shoulder of veal, cut into small pieces
- 50 ml extra virgin olive oil
- 1 T duck fat
- 3 carrots, peeled and sliced into pennies
- 16 whole baby onions, peeled
- 2 celery stalks with leaves, chopped
- 2 leeks, peeled and sliced into pennies
- 1 bouquet garni with rosemary, sage and thyme
- 2 bay leaves
- 3 cloves of garlic, peeled and chopped
- 400 ml pouring cream
- 5 egg yolks*
- juice of 2 lemons
- salt and freshly ground black pepper to taste

In a heavy saucepan, gently heat the olive oil and duck fat. Sauté the pieces of veal without colouring the meat. Add all the vegetables with the bouquet garni, bay leaves and garlic, and sauté together. Cover with water and cook over a low heat for at least 1 hour or until completely tender. Remove the meat and all the vegetables with a slotted spoon, cover and set aside in a warm place.

Strain the stock and return the liquid to the saucepan. Reduce over a medium heat with 100 ml of the cream to obtain a light, smooth sauce. Lightly whisk the rest of the cream and the egg yolks together, add to the stock off the heat (the sauce must not boil) and season to taste. Add the juice of the lemon and coat the meat with this sauce.

Serve with baby potatoes and a green salad.

* The five left-over egg whites, if whisked together with 350 g castor sugar and 1 t vanilla paste, will be perfect for a pile of little meringues!

RIGHT: *Entrance to Heaven.*

Chicken with sherry & cream

An all-time favourite dish that I sometimes cook with the lovely sherry-like wine from the Jura, Burgundy.

Serves 6

- 1 free-range chicken
- 50 g butter
- 50 ml extra virgin olive oil
- 3 leeks, sliced into pennies and washed
- 200 g button mushrooms
- 300 ml dry sherry
- 350 ml chicken stock
- 4 cloves of garlic, peeled
- 1 bouquet garni with parsley, rosemary, thyme and a bay leaf
- 300 ml pouring cream
- salt and pepper

Cut the chicken into 8 pieces.

In a casserole dish, sauté the chicken, skin side down, in a mixture of butter and olive oil before adding the leeks and button mushrooms. Braise lightly and add the sherry. Bring to a fast simmer and wait for the smell of alcohol to disappear before adding the chicken stock. The peeled garlic and bouquet garni can now go into the pot.

Cook on a low simmer for 45 minutes or until the meat is succulently done and the stock has reduced substantially. Add the pouring cream and cook for a further 15 minutes. Season with salt and pepper.

Place the chicken pieces on large platter, spoon over the creamy sauce and serve immediately.

TOP: *Owner Jacques Erasmus on the pass at Hemelhuijs.*
MIDDLE: *Having lunch at Hemelhuijs.*

Pork chops with port

This is a variation of an old recipe from the French countryside. I just love the richness of the sauce with a slice of freshly baked bread.

Serves 6

- 6 pork chops, sliced thickly
- 50 g flour
- 150 g butter
- 12 baby onions, peeled
- 25 g castor sugar
- 200 g smoked streaky bacon, chopped finely
- 500 g brown mushrooms, chopped finely
- 100 ml port
- 300 ml pouring cream
- salt and pepper

Flour the pork chops and sauté them in 50 g butter until they are well browned … about 6 minutes on each side. Keep warm in a moderate oven at 180 deg C/Gas 4.

Boil the onions in a little salted water until they are lightly cooked but still crunchy. Drain them, then add the sugar and 50 g of the butter to the pot and caramelise the onions over a fairly high heat.

In the meantime, melt the rest of the butter in a small pan, and braise the bacon and mushrooms until all the pan juices have been reduced completely. Deglaze the mixture with the port and add the cream. Cook gently for a further 10 minutes. Season the sauce to taste, spoon it over the pork chops and garnish with the caramelised onion.

Enjoy!

Let your dinner be a poem, like your dress.

CHARLES PIERRE MONSELET

TOP: *Victorian balcony at Keenwä.*

Quince crumble

It is also lovely to use apples for this dessert. They are ready for harvesting at the same time as quinces.

Serves 8

- 125 g butter
- 125 g sugar
- 1 egg
- 500 ml self-raising flour

Preheat the oven to 180 deg C/Gas 4.

Knead all the ingredients together into a soft, buttery ball. Wrap the dough gently in a piece of plastic and allow it to rest peacefully in the fridge for at least an hour. Butter a cookie tray. Remove the dough from the fridge and grate it with the roughest part of a grater to form coarse crumbs. I normally just grate the dough directly onto the cookie tray to form a thin layer. Bake the crumbs for about 25 minutes until golden.

Remove the tray from the oven and allow to cool completely before breaking the crumbs loose with your fingertips. They should be quite crunchy.

FILLING

- 4 medium quinces, halved
- 250 g sugar
- 2 cinnamon sticks
- 5 ml vanilla paste
- 1 T brandy
- 125 g raisins
- crème fraîche

Cover the quinces with cold water, add the sugar and cinnamon sticks and bring to a long, slow boil. Cook until soft, adding water if necessary. Remove the quinces from the pot and allow them to cool before peeling them. Cut into bite-sized slices. Reduce the lovely pink liquid until it has a syrupy consistency. Add the vanilla paste and brandy and pour over the quince slices.

Select 8 small, pretty glasses and spoon a tablespoonful of the crumbs into each of them. Fill them with the syrupy quince slices and raisins.

Garnish with a dollop of crème fraîche and serve.

... small helpings, no seconds, no snacking. And a little bit of everything.

JULIA CHILD

chapter 9

Market day

*S*aturday is market day in Woodstock. Best be at the Biscuit Mill with a large basket quite early. Begin your foray into food-heaven with a couple of freshly shucked oysters – and perhaps a small glass of ice-cold Cap Classique. Move on to a sumptuous eggs Benedict with crisp rosti, eaten at the endless communal trestle tables arranged all around the undercover market. You'll share it with market enthusiasts from all corners of the Peninsula. From Kalk Bay to Durbanville, they flock to share in the abundant produce.

And then you shop.

From the crustiest of breads to the creamiest of French cheeses. From fresh eggs to Jerusalem artichokes and tiny crisp green asparagus and handfuls of freshly cut basil and dill. Bunches of indigenous flowers. Bottles of truffle oil and pomegranate juice. Freshly caught fish and organic lamb.

A feast.

After this, it's off to the West Coast Market around the corner in Sir Lowry Road at The Palms. Stock your pantry with pickled mussels and purple Adam's figs. Lunch on vetkoek or prickly pears, with glorious cheesecake and rooibos tea or a bunch of grapes for afters, all wrapped in the warm hospitality of the people from the West Coast.

You'll travel home with so much more than the produce in your basket.

We are truly blessed.

MUSIC FOR THIS CHAPTER: *Dimanche En Hiver* by Keren Ann
OPPOSITE: *Fresh produce from the Saturday morning markets in Woodstock.*

- Vegetable soup with basil pesto

- Meatball sandwich with tomato sauce & Brie

- Veal kidneys in mustard sauce

- Green salad

- Asparagus with egg & caper mayonnaise

- Duck breast with blueberries

- Beef tongue with a white wine & port sauce

- Bread-and-butter pudding

Vegetable soup with basil pesto

I always love making a delicious soup using some basil pesto with it. Here is a really tasty recipe, one that will satisfy on most levels!

Serves 6

- 250 g bacon, sliced into small bits
- 1 T duck fat
- 500 g fresh green beans, trimmed and chopped finely
- 2 potatoes, peeled
- 2 carrots, peeled
- 2 leeks, peeled
- 500 g peas
- salt and pepper

BASIL PESTO
- 1 large bunch basil
- 3 cloves garlic, peeled
- 50 g pine nuts, roasted
- 50 g finely grated Parmesan cheese
- 200 ml extra virgin olive oil

In a soup casserole dish, melt the duck fat and braise the bacon bits lightly until the fat starts to run. Trim the green beans and chop them quite finely. Cut the potatoes, carrots and leeks into small cubes and add all the vegetables, including the peas, to the soup casserole dish. Cover the vegetables with twice their volume of water, bring to the boil and cook gently for 1 hour.

To make the pesto, crush the basil, garlic, pine nuts and Parmesan together with some of the olive oil, using a mortar and pestle or a handheld liquidiser until it forms a fabulous aromatic paste. Add the rest of the olive oil little by little, mixing all the time, until you have a thick, creamy paste.

To serve, spoon the soup into a bowl, add a dollop of pesto and enjoy!

ABOVE: *Vetkoek and Bella at the West Coast Market on Sir Lowry Road.*

RIGHT: Flammkuchen, *pizza* and saucisson *for sale at the Biscuit Mill Market on Albert Road, Woodstock.*

ABUNDANCE

Meatball sandwich with tomato sauce & Brie

How about this recipe? According to history it hails from Brisbane and is possibly one of the best subs I've eaten in my life! Real 'boy food'.

Serves 8

- 60 ml extra virgin olive oil
- 8 crusty white bread rolls
- 400 g ripe Brie, cut into 8 slices

MEATBALLS

- I slice white bread, crusts removed, soaked in water
- 500 g minced lamb*
- 125 g basil, chopped
- 125 g parsley, chopped
- 50 g mint, chopped
- I tomato, peeled, seeded and chopped finely
- I brown onion, peeled and grated
- 4 garlic cloves, peeled and chopped
- I egg, beaten
- salt and freshly ground black pepper to taste

TOMATO SAUCE

- 8 ripe tomatoes, peeled and chopped
- 60 ml extra virgin olive oil
- 4 garlic cloves, peeled
- I bay leaf
- I cinnamon stick
- I t dried basil
- I T castor sugar

Preheat the grill to medium.

For the meatballs, squeeze out the excess liquid from the bread and tear the bread into a large mixing bowl. Add the minced lamb, basil, parsley, mint, tomato, onion, garlic and egg, then mix vigorously to combine. Taste … yes, I know that it is raw … TASTE and season.

Cover and allow to rest in a cool place for at least 2 hours.

Roll the mixture into walnut-sized balls, place on a tray lined with baking paper and keep in the fridge until needed.

Meanwhile, for the sauce, heat the olive oil in a saucepan over a gentle heat and add the tomatoes, garlic, bay leaf, cinnamon, basil and sugar. Simmer this over a very low heat, stirring occasionally. This must be a thick, well-reduced paste-like sauce by the time you use it. Remove from the heat and keep warm.

Heat 60 ml olive oil in a sauce pan over medium heat. Add the meatballs and turn them occasionally until they are cooked through. Repeat the process until they are all done. Keep warm.

Place the bases of the rolls on an oven tray, divide the meatballs and place on the rolls, spoon the tomato sauce over the meat and place a slice of Brie on top. Grill in the oven until the cheese melts. Remove and top with the other half of the rolls.

Serve immediately!

* I ask my butcher for some. Just delicious!

Veal kidneys in mustard sauce

This is undeniably one of my favourite dishes. A little laborious to clean but just so worth the trouble!

Serves 4

- 500 g veal kidneys, cleaned and sliced in bite-sized pieces
- 1 T extra virgin olive oil
- 1 T butter
- 2 shallots, chopped finely
- 2 T brandy
- 150 ml thick cream
- 1 T creamy mustard
- salt and freshly ground black pepper

Heat the olive oil in a frying pan until really hot. Put the kidneys in the pan and sauté for about 6 minutes until they are lightly browned. Take care not to overcook them. Lift them from the pan with a spoon and keep in a warm dish.

Add the butter to the juices in the pan and heat well before adding the shallots to the pan for a quick sauté. Turn the heat up, add the brandy and simmer until the juice has reduced by half.

Add the cream and mustard and return the kidneys to the pan as well to reheat them gently. Taste, season and serve immediately with some crusty bread.

ABOVE: *Truffle oil and Pete Goffe-Wood's fabulous steak sandwiches at the Biscuit Mill.*

Luxury is not a necessity to me, but beautiful and good things are.

ANAÏS NIN

ABOVE: *Author breakfasting at the Biscuit Mill.*

Green salad

Possibly one of the simplest of salads … but if you get it just right, also one of the most delicious. It is based on a traditional French salad that is served on a piece of garlic-rubbed bread. By the time you get to the bread it has absorbed the garlic and the dressing. Fabulous!

Serves 6

- 125 ml extra virgin olive oil
- 1 t smooth mustard
- 1 t honey
- 1 t lemon juice, freshly squeezed
- 1 clove garlic, crushed
- 6 anchovies
- 150 g pine nuts, lightly roasted
- salt and white pepper to taste
- 6 handfuls of mixed young leaves and herbs, such as baby spinach, wild rocket, sorrel, basil, mint, chervil and flat-leaf parsley

In a large serving bowl, whisk together the olive oil, mustard, honey, lemon juice, garlic, anchovies and pine nuts. Taste and season.

Add the leaves to the bowl and toss well. You can serve this immediately.

It is wonderful with a plain omelette, a slice of crusty white bread and a glass of chilled white wine.

RIGHT: *Jewels from the sea at the West Coast Market.*

Asparagus with egg & caper mayonnaise

This is a lovely starter to serve in spring when asparagus is in season.

Serves 8

- 3 bunches young asparagus, rinsed really well
- 5 ml extra virgin olive oil
- 500 ml good quality mayonnaise
- 2 eggs, hardboiled, shelled and chopped
- 2 T capers, chopped
- 2 small gherkins, chopped
- zest of 1 lemon
- 1 t lemon juice
- salt and freshly ground black pepper

Blanch the asparagus in boiling water for 5 minutes and drain. Toss lightly with the olive oil.

Mix the mayonnaise, eggs, capers, gherkins, lemon zest and juice together with a spoon and taste.

Season with salt and freshly ground black pepper.

Serve the asparagus in little heaps on separate plates, each with a generous dollop of the egg and caper mayonnaise.

Duck breast with blueberries

To cook the meat beautifully you have to do it over a really low heat … the pan must be barely warm. And take your time!
I love to serve the duck breasts with a little cauliflower purée.

Serves 6

- 3 duck breasts
- a sprig each of sage, thyme and parsley, chopped finely
- salt and pepper to taste
- 300 ml red wine
- 3 shallots, peeled and chopped
- 100 ml crème de cassis
- 50 g butter, cut into small pieces
- 3 T blueberries

Use a sharp knife and score the skin and fat with five cuts per duck breast. Mix the chopped herbs with the salt and pepper and rub the mixture into the cuts.

Put a pan over a very low flame and place the duck breasts skin side down into the pan. The fat that will be released from the duck breasts will be sufficient to cook them in. Allow the meat to cook skin side down for about 30 minutes. Turn the meat, turn up the heat and quickly warm the other side of the meat for about 2 minutes. Slice the meat into thin slices and keep them warm on a serving platter.

In the meantime, bring the wine to the boil, add the shallots and reduce the wine by at least half before you add the crème de cassis. Reduce until the sauce has a shiny, syrupy consistency. Whisk the cold butter into the sauce, add the blueberries and spoon the sauce with the berries over the sliced duck breasts.

Serve with aplomb!

ABOVE: *Beautiful produce.*

Beef tongue WITH A WHITE WINE & PORT SAUCE

Another of my favourite variations to serve during the Christmas season.

Serves 6

- 1 beef tongue, preferably unpickled
- 3 carrots, peeled and sliced into pennies
- 2 onions, peeled and halved
- 3 celery stalks, chopped
- 1 bouquet garni, made with parsley, sage, a bay leaf and rosemary
- 2 shallots
- extra virgin olive oil
- 250 ml white wine
- 100 ml port
- 200 ml pouring cream
- 12 gherkins
- 1 T capers
- salt and pepper
- 1 T parsley, chopped

Immerse the tongue in a saucepan filled with water, bring to the boil and cook for about 20 minutes before adding the carrots, onions, celery and bouquet garni.

Cook for 3 hours or until the meat is very tender. Once the tongue is cooked, remove the skin and slice thinly in round slivers. Spoon a small amount of stock over the meat, cover and keep warm while you prepare the sauce.

Peel the shallots and chop them finely. In a pan, heat the olive oil and braise the shallots until they are well cooked and slightly browned. Deglaze the pan of shallots with white wine. Allow the wine liquid to reduce by half, add a ladleful of the cooking stock, then the port and cream. Allow to reduce very gently until the sauce has a smooth coating texture, then season to taste.

Slice the gherkins in really thin slices and add them to the sauce along with the capers. Cover the tongue slices with the sauce and garnish with a handful of chopped parsley.

Serve immediately with a heap of boiled and buttered baby potatoes.

FROM TOP DOWN: *Spotted at the Biscuit Mill: Luke Dawson and Lucas Rosenfield shopping; Off our feet; Luke Dale Roberts, chef extraordinaire; Market fare.*

MARKET DAY

Bread-and-butter pudding

This must be one of my all-time favourite desserts. An old classic that we have given the 'Italian-deli-just-around-the-corner' treatment. And it simply happened because a couple of years ago it was actually snowing on Table Mountain on Christmas Day. And we were in dire need of a baked pudding on Boxing Day!

Serves 6

- 6 eggs
- 300 ml full cream
- 300 ml milk
- 60 g castor sugar
- zest of an orange, very fine
- ½ t ground cinnamon
- 1 T vanilla paste
- 12 slices of panettone
- 60 g butter, unsalted
- 2 T brandy
- 2 T demerara sugar
- 1 T icing sugar
- 250 ml thick cream

Preheat the oven to 180 deg C/Gas 4.

Combine the eggs, cream, milk, castor sugar, orange zest, cinnamon and vanilla paste in a medium bowl and whisk really well to combine all the ingredients properly.

Spread both side of the slices of panettone with a thin smear of butter. Trim the cake slices to fit an ovenproof dish. Spoon the brandy over the cake and layer all the slices, sprinkling each layer with brandy as you go. Pour the cream mixture evenly over the layered, brandied slices and scatter the demerara sugar over the pudding.

Bake the pudding for about 35 minutes or until the custard has set and it has turned a mouth-watering golden colour.

Serve with a dusting of icing sugar and a large dollop of lusciously decadent thick cream.

Live to the point of tears. ALBERT CAMUS

chapter 10

Sailor in my kitchen

During the last couple of years a plethora of both serious and fabulously funky galleries, shops, bistros and small eateries have made an appearance in the trendier and more atmospheric areas that surround Table Bay. With generous friendliness, the most delicious food is being served to the young creatives of this city.

Exquisitely flavoured Indian food is being served at Chandani in Roodebloem Road, and delicious breads are being hauled out of the wood-burning ovens at The Artisan Baker in Albert Road. One of the best chefs in the country, Luke Dale Roberts, produces wonderful surprises at The Test Kitchen, and you can order perfectly ripe and runny cheeses from The Real Cheese in Lower Main Road. Hello Sailor in Observatory serves up charming breakfasts over the road from the well-known theatre and Obz Café where many a story has been told and retold.

And then there are generous platefuls of home-cooked meals served with the warmth of welcoming a long-lost family member at The Kitchen in Sir Lowry Road; and quiet family breakfasts over the road at The Deli.

A feast of bistros and restaurants like a string of jewels is strung along the perimeter of the Cape Town harbour.

Our lovely city.

MUSIC FOR THIS CHAPTER: *Turista Accidental* by Amparo Sánchez
OPPOSITE: *Obz Café and theatre in Observatory.*

- Lemon & chilli guacamole

- Piperade with peppers

- Onion & Gruyère tart

- Salade Niçoise

- Chicken with olives

- Christina's Kalk Bay lamb casserole

- Fruit mince tea slices

- Berry trifle

Lemon & chilli guacamole

The world changed for me the first time I ate chilli. This is the easiest and most pleasant way to get shot of all those extra avocados.

Serves 6

- 6 avocados, flesh sliced elegantly into rounds
- 2 brown onions, peeled and sliced
- 100 g fresh coriander leaves
- 2 T lemon, freshly squeezed
- 4 T extra virgin olive oil
- 4 green chillies, chopped
- 4 cloves of garlic, peeled and sliced thinly

Arrange the avocado slices beautifully on a large serving dish.

Garnish with the onion slices and the coriander leaves.

In a separate bowl, whisk the lemon juice, olive oil, chillies and garlic together.

Spoon the sauce over the avocado and serve with warm crusty bread.

ABOVE: *The Deli on Sir Lowry Road.*

If you are afraid of butter, use cream.   JULIA CHILD

Piperade with peppers

What a deliciously messy snack this is … one of those that you need to eat outside, leaning forward with feet slightly apart … heaven forbid that you should mess on your shoes! I just love serving this with some crusty bread before a meal.

Serves 6

- 4 red peppers
- 4 green peppers
- 4 yellow peppers
- 4 ripe tomatoes
- 6 cloves garlic
- 4 shallots or small leeks
- 150 ml extra virgin olive oil
- 1 T parsley, chopped
- 1 T thyme, stems removed and lightly chopped

ABOVE: *Favourite Friday night Indian dinners on Roodebloem Road, Woodstock.*

Put on the grill and roast all the peppers in the oven for 20 minutes, turning them regularly. Allow them to cool down and peel them. Make sure that you painstakingly remove all the pips. Do not be tempted to rinse them though! You will only succeed in washing off the fabulously tasty juices that have been released by the roasting process!

Slice the peppers into thin strips. Blanch, peel and chop the tomatoes. Peel the garlic and shallots (or the leeks) and chop them finely. Add olive oil to the peppers, tomatoes, garlic and shallots, and gently poach them together in a casserole dish on the stove for about 10 minutes.

Spoon the piperade into a serving dish and garnish with the chopped parsley and thyme.

Serve with fresh bread as a starter.

Onion & Gruyère tart

This is a variation on the well-known pissaladière.
I suspect most of us have the odd friend or two who becomes quite grumpy if he is hungry … this recipe
helps a lot in these cases! I often serve this as a quick snack when guests arrive.
Serves 8

- 1 roll of puff pastry, defrosted
- 50 g butter
- 3 eggs, one of which must be separated
- 1 T extra virgin olive oil
- 3 brown onions, peeled and sliced into thin rings
- 10 sprigs thyme, chopped finely
- salt and freshly ground pepper to taste
- 125 ml cream
- 50 g Parmesan, freshly grated
- 150 g Gruyère, grated finely
- 8 anchovies

Preheat the oven to 180 deg C/Gas 4.

Lightly butter a loose-bottomed pan and line with the puff pastry. Brush the pastry case with egg white and allow it to rest in the fridge.*

Heat the olive oil and the rest of the butter in a pan and fry the onion until it is translucent and quite soft. Sprinkle the thyme over the onion.

Add the separated egg yolk to the rest of the eggs and beat the eggs and cream together with a fork before adding the Parmesan and Gruyère cheeses to the mixture. Slide the cooked onions into the mix, season, and then fold all the ingredients gently together.

Remove the pastry case from the fridge. Spoon the onion and cheese mixture onto the pastry and bake the tart for about 25 minutes or until the pastry has puffed up nicely and is a lovely caramel colour.

Garnish the tart with the anchovies and serve with a green salad.

*This will prevent the pastry from becoming soggy.

RIGHT: *Food and wine moments at Luke Dale Robert's The Test Kitchen at the Biscuit Mill.*

Salade Niçoise

After the very long flight from Cape Town to Paris, this is the one meal I always order while waiting for the train to the middle of France.
Recently I've started to serve this for friends in Cape Town on a regular basis. It is so good!

Serves 6

- 300 g tuna in oil, drained and shredded
- 24 marinated anchovies, whole
- 30 black olives
- 6 medium-boiled eggs, quartered
- 1 red pepper, sliced in rings
- 48 whole green beans, blanched lightly
- 6 tomatoes, quartered
- 1 red onion, sliced thinly
- 50 ml extra virgin olive oil
- sea salt and freshly ground pepper

These are the basic ingredients of a salade niçoise. Add any raw vegetables you like, such as cucumber or green lettuce. Serve the salad with a dribble of olive oil, a little salt and pepper, the sound of the sea and the deed is done!

Serve individually on breakfast plates as a starter or on one huge platter.

Karen Dudley's welcoming Kitchen in Sir Lowry Road, Woodstock.

ABOVE: *Breakfast at Hello Sailor in Observatory.*

Chicken with olives

Another one of our favourite Cape summer throw-in-the-pan chicken dishes. This is very good with some slices of fresh, crusty bread to mop up the sumptuous sauce.

Serves 6

- 6 chicken thighs
- 6 chicken legs
- 125 ml olive oil
- 1 T duck fat
- 8 shallots, peeled and chopped finely
- 5 cloves garlic, peeled
- 40 large green olives, stoned
- handful sage and thyme, finely chopped
- 125 ml dry white wine
- 2 bay leaves
- 6 leeks, sliced into pennies and washed
- 1 L chicken stock*
- handful fresh basil, roughly chopped

Heat 75 ml of the olive oil and the duck fat in a large pan. Add the shallots and braise until soft. Remove from the pan and use a handheld blender to purée them with the raw garlic, half of the olives, half the chopped herb mixture and the rest of the olive oil.

Fry the chicken pieces in the same pan and remove when nicely browned. Keep warm. Add the wine to the pan and deglaze the bits and pieces over a high heat. Reduce all the juices almost completely before scraping the purée into the pan. Return the warm chicken pieces to the pan together with the rest of the herbs, bay leaves and leeks.

Pour in the stock and cook for about 35 minutes until the chicken is tender and the liquid has reduced a little. Add the rest of the olives and cook for another 10 minutes.

Remove the cooked chicken pieces from the pan and keep warm on a serving platter. Reduce the sauce further until it has an almost creamy consistency.

Stir the freshly chopped basil into the sauce and spoon over the chicken.

Serve with a mound of steaming basmati rice.

* See recipe on page 71.

Christina's Kalk Bay lamb casserole

Without a doubt one of the best happy meals I have ever had! I hope you all love it as much as my family does …

Serves 10

- 1.6 kg leg of lamb, oven-roasted, deboned and sliced
- 50 ml extra virgin olive oil
- 8 ripe tomatoes, peeled and chopped
- 1 T dried basil
- 6 cloves garlic, peeled and chopped
- 6 leeks, sliced into pennies and washed well
- 3 aubergines, sliced and fried in extra virgin olive oil
- 500 g feta cheese, crumbled
- 250 g black olives, pitted
- 550 ml thick, creamy béchamel, freshly made
- 1 egg
- 1 T oregano, freshly chopped or dried

Preheat the oven to 180 deg C/Gas 4.

Butter a large ovenproof casserole dish.

Heat the olive oil in a saucepan and sauté the tomatoes, basil, garlic and leeks in the oil over medium heat until well cooked and all the flavours are properly infused. Keep aside.

In the casserole dish, start with a layer of the sliced lamb. Follow with a layer of aubergine with a layer of the tomato mixture on top. Sprinkle with some of the crumbled feta and oregano. Repeat, starting again with the lamb. Try to finish with a layer of aubergine and add a layer of olives to finish. Whisk the egg into the béchamel before pouring the sauce over and through the meat and vegetable dish. Place the casserole dish in the heated oven and bake uncovered for 40 minutes.

Remove from the oven and garnish with the freshly chopped oregano. Serve immediately with steaming basmati rice.

BÉCHAMEL SAUCE
For a good béchamel, you need a spoonful or two of butter, melted. Stir the same amount of flour into the butter, adding milk as you stir. Keep going until you have a lovely creamy white sauce. Season the sauce and use as required.

LEFT: *The still fabulous Obz Café and theatre.*

Fruit mince tea slices

*Instead of skipping off to your local grocery store to go shopping for some fruit mince pies,
try to bake these. They are utterly sumptuous and really no effort.*

16 slices

- 1 roll of puff pastry, defrosted
- 250 g fruit mince
- 25 g pistachios, slightly crushed
- 50 g almonds, chopped
- 50 g dried cranberries, chopped
- 50 g dried cherries, sugared and chopped
- 75 g icing sugar
- 3 T lemon juice

Heat the oven to 200 deg C/Gas 6.

In a mixing bowl, combine the fruit mince, pistachios, almonds, cranberries and cherries. Open the pastry and place the rolled sheet of pastry on a greased baking tray. Carefully spread the fruit mince mixture right to the edges of the pastry.

Bake for about 20 minutes or until the pastry has a lovely caramel colour. Remove from the oven and leave to cool.

Use 50 g of the icing sugar and whisk with the lemon juice to form a thin syrup. Drizzle this over the cool pastry and slice into 16 slices.

Dust with the remaining icing sugar and serve.

Everything in moderation ... including moderation.   JULIA CHILD

ABOVE: *The Artisan Baker.*

Berry trifle

This is a deliciously light dessert that I love to serve in small individual portions. Just a little something sweet after a summer lunch. And it looks really festive.

Serves 8

- 500 ml mascarpone
- 1 T icing sugar, sifted
- 1 t vanilla paste
- 200 ml cream, whipped
- 200 g castor sugar
- 150 ml water
- 1 gelatine leaf
- 100 g strawberries, hulled
- ½ loaf of sponge cake, sliced about 5 mm thick and cut to fit in the bottom of a small glass
- 2 T sweet sherry
- 50 g blueberries
- 50 g raspberries

Combine the mascarpone and icing sugar in a bowl. Add the vanilla and fold gently together. Add the whipped cream.

Use a small pan and dissolve the sugar in the water. Add the gelatine as well as the strawberries and simmer for about 5 minutes, stirring constantly. Remove from the heat and liquidise. Allow to cool to room temperature.

Make individual servings in 8 glasses by placing a layer of the sponge cake in the bottom of each glass. Spoon a little sherry on top of each round of cake. Drop a mixture of the berries into each glass, drizzle with the strawberry purée and spoon a dollop of mascarpone on top. Repeat the layering, finishing with a small scattering of berries.

Place all 8 glasses on a tray and leave them in the fridge until you need to serve them.

THIS PAGE: *Shopping in Albert Road.*

ACKNOWLEDGEMENTS

I wrote this book for everybody who has ever left me slightly breathless.

Firstly I want to thank photographer Johan Wilke for his take on our wonderful city. And his wry sense of humour while we were shooting the ongoing stream of food pictures. It was a pleasure to work with you.

For inspiration and a deft hand in the kitchen, thank you Alet Steenkamp. Also my dear friend Joyce Melane, who always knows how to keep a cool head, and her assistant Nonni Ranemane – I thank you both.

Thanks to Louise Hennigs who opened her lovely home for us. My thanks also go to all the very generous restaurant owners and chefs of Cape Town who welcomed us so warmly into their bistros and kitchens.

To Basil van Rooyen and Terry Morris: thank you for publishing and distributing this book. It is and will always be a privilege to have anything in print.

Louise Grantham, my long-suffering and supremely patient publisher, thank you so much.

Thank you, Jane Macduff, for the thankless task of proofreading all the recipes and putting up with my endless, dark mutterings. I really appreciate your gracious enthusiasm during this ordeal. Thank you, René de Wet, for your artistic hand in the design of *Abundance*.

Also thanks to Heather Parker who, as always, helped me with some copy-editing.

A special thank you to our son, Renier, for his creative input. It is much appreciated!

And to my dearest friend and husband Deon, I raise a glass of slightly chilled Pinot Noir.

Marlene van der Westhuizen

GLOSSARY

aioli – garlic mayonnaise

al dente – still slightly chewy, not too soft

al fresco – in the fresh air, outside

bain-marie – pan with simmering water with a bowl suspended in it

béchamel – white sauce made with butter, flour, milk and seasoning

bourride – a Provençal fish soup; after cooking the liquid is strained and traditionally bound with aioli or eggs

Boursin® – a garlic-and-herb flavoured cream cheese with crushed peppercorns

chèvre – cheese made from goat's milk

crème fraîche – a cream to which a lactic acid has been added which thickens the cream and gives it a distinctive sharp flavour without souring the cream

Crottin – a strong-flavoured goat's milk cheese, small and hard in texture

demerara sugar – light-brown cane sugar

fasolia – a hearty Lebanese red or white bean dish with lots of spices and chilli

frangipane – almond cream

French-trimmed – a method used to trim the fat and muscle from the rib so the bone is revealed, e.g. rack of lamb

gratin – a shallow, ovenproof dish used to brown a grated cheese and breadcrumb (optional) topping under a grill

mascarpone – a thick, creamy Italian cheese often used in desserts

muscovado sugar – a partially refined sugar that is sticky, soft and brown in colour

panettone – Italian cake made of nuts, spices, sultanas and candied peel, raised with yeast

pissaladière – French-type of pizza

Reblochon – a mild, buttery flavoured, high fat French cheese made from cow's milk, shaped like Camembert without the runny consistency

rillette – similar to a pâté, it is a preparation of pork, rabbit, goose, game or poultry, deboned and cooked in lard and then pounded to a smooth paste, potted and served as a cold snack

roux – equal amounts of melted butter and flour used to make or thicken sauces

sauce vierge – a French sauce usually served with fish; made from olive oil and a variety of herbs and vegetables but most commonly olive oil, garlic, lemon juice, chopped tomato and basil

scaloppini – veal or poultry cutlets that have been pounded thin, coated in flour and sautéed

serranito – a popular warm sandwich originally from Andalusia, Spain made usually of grilled meat, cured ham, tomato and fried green peppers

tagliolini pasta – a traditional type of pasta that is cut in long, flat and really thin ribbons

tapenade – a paste made of cured black olives, seasoned with olive oil, garlic, anchovies, capers and lemon

tartiflette – a traditional dish from the Haute Savoie region in France made with potatoes, Reblochon cheese, cream and bacon fat

velouté – a basic sauce made with chicken or veal stock and thickened with a roux

ANATOLI'S
24 Napier Street, Green Point
+27 21 419 2501

ARIS SOUVLAKI
83A Regent Road, Sea Point
+ 27 21 439 6683

THE ARTISAN BAKER
399 Albert Road, Woodstock
+ 27 21 447 5293

BIZERCA BISTRO
15 Anton Anreith Arcade,
Jetty Street, Cape Town, Foreshore
+27 21 418 0001

CAFÉ MANHATTAN
74 Waterkant Street,
De Waterkant
+27 21 421 6666

CAFÉ MOZART
37 Church Street, Cape Town
+27 21 424 3774

CHANDANI
85 Roodebloem Road, Woodstock
+27 21 447 7887

THE DELI
190 Sir Lowry Road, Woodstock
+27 21 461 8056

FORK
84 Long Street, Cape Town
+27 21 424 6334

FRENCH TOAST
199 Bree Street, Cape Town
+27 21 422 3839

GIOVANNI'S
103 Main Road, Green Point
+27 21 434 6893

GOLD RESTAURANT
96 Strand Street, Cape Town
+27 21 421 4653

HAAS
67 Rose Street, Bo Kaap
+27 21 422 4413

HELLO SAILOR
122b Lower Main Road,
Observatory

HEMELHUIJS
72 Waterkant Street,
City Bowl
+27 21 418 2042

JASON BAKERY
185 Bree Street, Cape Town
+27 21 424 5644

KEENWÄ
50 Waterkant Street, City Bowl
+27 21 419 2633

THE KITCHEN
111 Sir Lowry Road, Woodstock
+27 21 462 2201

LA BOHEME WINE BAR & BISTRO
341 Main Road, Sea Point
+27 21 434 8797

LA PERLA
Beach Road, Sea Point
+27 21 434 2471

LA PETITE TARTE
Cape Quarter, Waterkantstraat 72,
De Waterkant
+27 21 425 9077

LOADING BAY
30 Hudson Street, De Waterkant
+27 21 425 6320

MANO'S
107 Main Road, Green Point
+27 21 434 1090

MARCO'S AFRICAN PLACE
71 Wale Street, Bo Kaap
+27 21 423 5412

MAREMOTO
230 Long Street, Cape Town
+27 21 422 5877

MINATO SUSHI RESTAURANT
4 Buiten Street, Cape Town
+27 21 423 4712

OBZ CAFÉ
115 Lower Main Road, Observatory
+27 21 448 5555

ORIGIN
28 Hudson Street, De Waterkant
+27 21 421 1000

PIZZERIA NAPOLETANA
Main Road, Sea Point
+27 21 434 5386

THE REAL CHEESE
217 Lower Main Road,
Observatory
+27 21 448 8041

ROYALE EATERY
273 Long Street, Cape Town
+27 21 422 4536

SKINNY LEGS & ALL
70 Loop Street, Cape Town
+27 21 423 5403

THE SLUG & LETTUCE
107A Main Road, Green Point
+27 21 433 2081

SOCIETI BISTRO
50 Orange Street, Gardens
+27 21 424 2100

THE TEST KITCHEN
Old Biscuit Mill
375 Albert Road, Woodstock
+27 21 447 2337

ZUCCHINI RESTAURANT
83 Loop Street, Cape Town
+27 21 424 8571

INDEX

ISBN: 978-1-920434-44-1

First edition, first impression 2012

Published jointly by Bookstorm (Pty) Limited, Suite 10, Private Bag X12, Cresta 2118, Johannesburg, South Africa, www.bookstorm.co.za and Pan Macmillan South Africa, Private Bag X19, Northlands 2116, Johannesburg, South Africa, www.panmacmillan.co.za

Distributed by Pan Macmillan
Via Booksite Afrika

Edited by Pat Botes
Proofread by Pat Botes and Aïda Thorne
Cover and book design by René de Wet
Typeset by René de Wet
Photographs by Johan Wilke
Printed by Ultra Litho